The Current of
Romantic Passion

The Current
of Romantic
Passion

Jeffrey C. Robinson

The University of
Wisconsin Press

The University of Wisconsin Press
114 North Murray Street
Madison, Wisconsin 53715

3 Henrietta Street
London WC2E 8LU, England

5   4   3   2   1

Printed in the United States of America

Library of Congress Cataloging-in-Publication Data
Robinson, Jeffrey Cane, 1943–
The current of romantic passion / Jeffrey C. Robinson.
214 pp.   cm.
Includes bibliographical references and index.
ISBN 0-299-12960-8 ISBN 0-299-12964-0 (pbk.)
1. Romanticism.   2. European literature—18th century—History and
criticism.   3. European literature—19th century—History
and criticism.   I. Title.
PN603.R54   1991
809'.9145—dc20   91-6580
CIP

For Beth

. . . whoever at his death leaves behind one beautiful line of verse leaves the skies and the earth richer and the reason for there being stars and people more emotionally mysterious.

—Fernando Pessoa

Let, let the amorous burn—
But, prithee, do not turn
The current of your heart from me so soon. . . .

—John Keats

Protest that endures, I think, is moved by a hope far more modest than that of public success: namely, the hope of preserving qualities in one's own heart and spirit that would be destroyed by acquiescence.

—Wendell Berry

{ Contents }

[*Acknowledgments*]

This book, though possibly brief in the reading, was long in the gestating and the making. It represents my concern about what might be called the trouble of beauty in (primarily Romantic) literature and as such calls attention to my struggle—a skepticism, impatience, and longing—with the possibility and desirability of transcendence and spirituality in the Romantic work of art and in one's response to it. This struggle in me has not abated. Nor does this book represent any particular peace with the subject, but it is for the moment a landing place. It seems, therefore, a good opportunity to acknowledge those persons who have over the past several years contributed in greater or lesser degrees to my understanding of the nature and function of Romantic art: Marilyn Butler, Beth Darlington, Sidney Goldfarb, William Keach, James R. Kincaid (who has read the manuscript in full and given unfailing and informed encouragement), Marilyn Krysl, Marjorie Levinson (in *Keats's Life of Allegory*), Jane Lilienfeld, Peter Manning, Jerome McGann, Gerda Norvig, Elizabeth Robertson, David Simpson, and an anonymous reader for the University of Wisconsin Press. As he was with an earlier book of mine, *Radical Literary Education*, the Press's director Allen Fitchen has been unusually supportive and patient with this book and its author whose other commitments at times delayed completion.

The material in several sections—those on Dorothy Wordsworth, Wordsworth's late poetry about women, and Coleridge and Thelwall—was presented in substantially different form at the MLA conventions of 1984, 1985, and 1986. The parts of Section 1, on Shelley's *Epipsychidion*, and on Hazlitt's "The Fight" were given in altered form at a conference on Romanticism and the French Revolution, in Rome, 1989.

Thanks go to the University of Colorado Council on Research and Creative Work for granting me a Faculty Fellowship during the year 1986–87 to work uninterruptedly on this project, and to Colleen Anderson and Vincine Sanchez who quickly typed the book into presentable form.

Finally I would like to thank my parents, Arthur and Mary Robinson, for their generous and loving support—in professional and personal endeavors—over many years.

The Current of
Romantic Passion

[1]

Romanticism, and Passion,

and Beauty

The major Victorian critics of Romantic writers perceived, much more than do most twentieth-century readers, the Romantic preoccupation with desire and passion. Matthew Arnold was emphatic in his assessment of Keats as a poet, and a person, of great, indeed too much, passion. Keats's letters to Fanny Brawne indicate his limitation as a poet because of it. Walter Pater described Lamb as a writer "content, all his life, with pure brotherliness, . . . in place of the *passion* of love." Wordsworth, says Pater, though his own character had "a sort of inborn religious placidity," "was able to appreciate passion in the lowly." "The great distinguishing passion came to Michael by the sheepfold, to Ruth by the wayside, adding these humble children of the furrow to the true aristocracy of passionate souls." [1] In America the Columbia professor George Edward Woodberry, speaking in 1903 about Wordsworth, said:

> When you go out to walk alone in a scene of natural beauty, your senses are first excited and interested; but often there arise in consequence feelings and ideas harmonious with the scene, and emotionally touched with it, which gradually absorb your consciousness; and at last you find yourself engaged in a mood—perhaps of memory—from which the external scene has entirely dropped away or round which it is felt only as a nimbus or halo of beauty, or mystery or calm. [2]

The feeling of a "nimbus or halo of beauty," a "calm," replaces the external scene and the accompanying excitement. Now it is true that Arnold criticizes Keats for a passion that kept the poet from attaining the rare heights of a tragically disinterested poetry. And it is true that Pater appreciates Lamb's preference or capacity for brotherliness over passionate love and that the passions of Wordsworth's characters reflect or define an essential self, a rocklike position in society and not the wayward energies of desire. Nonetheless passion often seems to lie at the center of the Victorians' efforts at understanding their Romantic predecessors.

In the major twentieth-century discussions of Romanticism, readers have tended not to consider passion and desire very important. Romantic poetry seems to have defined the literary activity of the period, a poetry that is typically described in terms of the achievement of identity or self-realization and as such as being more interested in the final coalescence of "self" than in the representations of passion and desire along the way. Marilyn Butler's *Romantics, Rebels, and Reactionaries* (1982) and Jerome McGann's *The Romantic Ideology* (1983) have referred to the importance of the representation of erotic passion in, particularly, the poetry of the younger Romantic generation in England. Unlike Arnold and Pater, Butler and McGann and several other more recent feminist critics associate the representation of erotic passion with radical or reformist tendencies in Romanticism, in the line of Blake.

In this book I propose that the drama of passion, in fiction and essays as well as poetry, may be more representative of Romantic literature than the drama of an internalized, reflexive consciousness in an idyllic setting. The centrality of passion and desire in a paradigm of the Romantic poem destabilizes our definition of beauty and our evaluation of it. To demonstrate this I will consider works not ordinarily viewed as staples of the Romantic canon and will emphasize in the canonical writings unfamiliar elements and ways of reading.

When he asserts in *The Reveries of the Solitary Walker* that the "ideal occupation [botany] has a charm which can only be felt when the passions are at rest,"[3] Rousseau appears to speak as an old man who, having judged his life a series of exhausting battles and wearisome emotional entanglements, seeks at the end a little calm. Attenuate those enervating passions, says Rousseau, with which I engage and am engaged by society and I will uncover "the sentiment of existence," the nearly physiological feeling and desire of mere living. But the cultivation of this extreme, benign, calming sentiment does not only belong to Rousseau's final years; his book *Emile* (1762) gauged the success of the ideal education of the modern person by how well he or she can subdue passion or divert it from either objects of erotic interest or occasions for social critique. When a young adolescent male hints at a potential passion for a young woman, for example, he ought to be encouraged to go out hunting for rabbits instead. In his later years Rousseau perceived social passion and erotic desire as being personally and politically dangerous as well as painful and aggravating. By attaching so much importance to them, he deeply understood, and also helped to establish, one of the major preoccupations of writers in the next fifty years and beyond. In my view "passion" is one of those obvious subjects in Romantic writing that modern readers have neglected.

By "passion" I mean primarily erotic passion and desire. The representation of erotic passion in eighteenth-century novels and plays usually anticipates social, domestic destabilization. Conversely that potential disruption is responded to as if it were an intrusion upon the body and the mind of the individual person. Literary representations of passion roughly divide between those in which passion is deplored, rationalized, suppressed, diverted, or transcended and those in which passion is equivalent to joy and to the limits of knowledge and human possibility, as in Blake's Proverb of Hell: "You never know what is enough until you know what is more than enough." Moreover, erotic passion and the passion for liberty, that is, the energy, perceived by Blake in *Visions of the Daughters of Albion* as driving the radicals in the French Revolution, are the same thing.

Imagine a history or a profile of the characteristic Romantic poem that, instead of resembling Wordsworth's "Tintern Abbey," with its celebration of the contemplative mind at ease in the countryside, is modeled on Blake's *Visions of the Daughters of Albion*, at least on the following passage from it, as Oothoon, full of sexual desire, plucks the flower/nymph Marygold:

> I pluck thee from thy bed
> Sweet flower and put thee here to glow between my breasts
> And thus I turn my face to where my whole soul seeks.
> Over the waves she went in wing'd exulting swift delight;
> And over Theotormons reign, took her impetuous course.
> Bromion rent her with his thunders on his stormy bed
> Lay the faint maid, and soon her woes appalld his thunders hoarse.[4]

The expression of Oothoon's innocent sexual desire produces its suppression in Bromion's reign of terror. For Blake, particularly during the years of the French Revolution, the primary moral issue is the fate of desire—its flowering or its containment. This passage, or the Argument to the poem rehearsing essentially the same sorrow, contrasts with the illustration of the Argument in which the beautiful, naked Oothoon kisses the naked human form of the Marygold as it dances or flies by, as in Blake's aphoristic quatrain:

> He who binds to himself a joy
> Does the winged life destroy

> But he who kisses the joy as it flies
> Lives in eternity's sun rise.[5]

If these passages are my model, then Romantic poetry and more generally Romantic literature enunciate the tension of erotic passion in the Revolutionary and post-Revolutionary period. I am alive to its possible suppression as I am to its possible release.

Poems are presences. They have no reason for being other than their immediacy for us. In a world where most experience seems displaced and mediated, poetry can isolate the reader or listener before his or her god, before the "voice" or the "image" of the person. In our world poetry occasions a unique possibility for intimacy, for conscious intimacy. Poetry should be "better" than ordinary life. Prophetic poetry shapes that intimacy as a cry from the private person to the civic consciousness. In our world the poetic spirit is that which touches the private person, and I call it "the beautiful." It is that which allows me to hold my private experience with poetry to myself, that which confirms by its own coherence of form and resolution the boundaries of my own being. It has always been claimed by theories of the beautiful that it marks one's sense of order, unity, harmony, and transcendence, and that it acknowledges the possibility of affirmation of spirit. We fill the experience of the beautiful with pleasure.

It is nearly impossible today to speak without irony or deprecation about the beautiful. That which dominated discussion in philosophy and aesthetics for centuries now appears a phantom concept, its power unfelt. It is a shade of the millennia of idealism. It, like Freud's religion, is an illusion; perhaps it is the experience of the *aura* described by Walter Benjamin, that distancing glow surrounding the original artwork from before the age of mechanical reproduction; or perhaps it is the elegiac glow that Lionel Trilling found in Keats's urn, with "pastness as one of its attributes." Or it may be that "beauty" defines and affirms the experience of that secular "soul" produced in industrial capitalism, a space demanding for its existence an agreement to maintain social conditions as they are—the opposite of "mind," that which asserts the necessity to irritate the present into social change. But today in the universities at least, it casts so faint a light that it hardly needs demystification.

Academic Marxist and feminist literary studies have effaced the beautiful, finding it by implication if not openly a phenomenon created or promoted by capitalism or by the masculine bias in literary production. These

days it simply seems irrelevant to the more pressing concerns of history
and gender. As a corrective to the tired assumptions of the academy about
methods of reading, emphases on interpretations, and what books deserve
reading, Marxism and feminism are invaluably liberating and intellectually
exciting, but the relegation of the idea of the beautiful to the backwater
seems to me deeply mistaken and at times an arrogant gesture. Moreover,
this dismissal reinforces an American myopia about the beautiful: What
does the mainstream culture promote as beautiful? Anything? Does the
concept register with the population at large? One suspects, for example,
that in Italy Botticelli's *La Primavera* would be called "beautiful"; that
schoolchildren would be taught that it was beautiful. Not that one would
have to accept the view that *La Primavera* is beautiful; but a *conventional* instance of beauty would exist, and therefore one would have to *contend* with
beauty as part of ordinary cultural experience. I cannot think of something
comparable in America.

In denying ourselves the beautiful, we have lost in addition the erotic
experience that accompanies our access to it and our experience of it. This,
in a society as neurotic about desire as ours, should come as no surprise.
But we can see the separation of the beautiful from the erotic and the preference for the former over the latter in the Victorian period, in the essays of
Arnold on Keats and Pater on Lamb. One can return further to the Romantic period itself and see in some of the reviews of Keats's 1817 volume the
deprecation of the sensuous elements in his poetic language as embodying
the fundamental wish to separate beauty from the erotic. Or, as Tolstoy
says in summing up eighteenth- and nineteenth-century aestheticians on
the beautiful: "the reception by us of a certain kind of pleasure, *i.e.* we call
'beauty' that which pleases us without evoking in us desire." [6]

Recalling the first discussions of beauty in Western philosophy, Plato's
in the *Phaedrus* and the *Symposium*, we realize that originally beauty was
not separated from desire. In the *Phaedrus* one desires beauty in the same
way that a man desires a lover, and who can forget the description?—"at
first a shudder runs through him, and again the old awe steals over him;
then looking upon the face of his beloved as of a god he reverences him,
and if he were not afraid of being thought a downright madman, he would
sacrifice to his beloved as to the image of a god; then while he gazes on
him there is a sort of reaction, and the shudder passes into an unusual heat
and perspiration . . ." [7] This passage ought to make us halt before modern
cavalier and not-so-cavalier dismissals of beauty. It may be that beauty is

an idealist fantasy of completeness, granted only or primarily to men and to the well-to-do, but that such intensity should be granted the experience of the beautiful by Plato ought to make us suspect that our dismissal probably will come at a considerable human price. Are we denying or suppressing an important dimension of experience?

If Plato belongs to the too distant past, then turn to the modern Mexican poet Octavio Paz: ". . . the poem is a means of access to pure time, an immersion in the original waters of existence." Here the beauty of the poem evokes a spirituality that is primary, in a language of ritual purification that does not exclude erotic desire. For Paz this spirituality *is* erotic. Of Romantic poets he says they "have set against the linear time of progress and of history the instantaneous time of eroticism. . . ."[8] His "erotic" corresponds to the idealist's "beautiful"—timeless, ahistorical. In this Paz differs little from Blake: "He who kisses the joy as it flies / Lives in eternity's sunrise."

How can we account for the preferred separation of beauty and erotic desire in the dominant European and American culture after the French Revolution? In Herbert Marcuse's classic 1937 essay, "The Affirmative Character of Culture," beauty has become attached to the "soul," which, since the Renaissance, marks out the space—separate from the reality of social labor—in which all non-labor-related experience resides. The world of labor becomes the "bad present," the site of oppression and exploitation. For those not oppressed, beauty can be acquired as a mark of one's freedom from oppression, one's triumph over it. Beauty embodies the freedom and dignity of the "soul," which, however, demands the suppression of eros and mind. Mind is that which connotes a different freedom: the freedom to criticize the dominating elements of society and potentially to effect change in them. Eros, or desire, becomes the energy for critical activity, for the autonomy of the individual. Thus for Marcuse the Kantian association of beauty with disinterestedness strips beauty of its social and personal vitality. Mind becomes marginal to the dominant culture, and eros becomes instead part of the bad present and sinks beneath the pure serene of beauty.

Yet beauty can be perceived quite differently: beauty contains a dangerous violence that threatens the given form of existence. The immediate sensuousness of beauty immediately suggests sensuous happiness. According to Hume the power to stimulate pleasure belongs to the essential character of beauty. Pleasure is not merely a by-product of beauty, but constitutes its very essence. And for Nietzsche beauty reawakens "aphrodisiac bliss." He polemicizes against Kant's definition of the beautiful as the object of completely disinterested pleasure (*Wohlgefallen*) and opposes to it Stendhal's assertion that beauty is "une promesse de bonheur." Therein lies its danger in a society that must rationalize and regulate happiness. Beauty is fundamentally shameless.[9]

In his more recent book, *The Aesthetic Dimension: Toward a Critique of Marxist Aesthetics* (1978), Marcuse develops the discussion of beauty as part of a progressive political program, and—following Nietzsche and Stendhal—can speak to the "radical potential" through the "erotic quality of the Beautiful": "As pertaining to the domain of eros, the beautiful represents the pleasure principle. Thus, it rebels against the prevailing reality principle of domination. The work of art speaks the liberating language, invokes the liberating images of the subordination of death and destruction to the will to live. This is the emancipatory element in aesthetic affirmation."[10]

A cultural artifact in bourgeois society, it follows, supports the spiritual freedom of the dominant classes and affirms their perpetuation when it registers the suppression or disarming of erotic desire. Here what is implicit in Marcuse becomes explicit in Michel Foucault who sees modern, post-Enlightenment culture as dedicated to the control of disruptive desire, not by the latter's suppression but by its expression. Its very visibility in the appropriate setting denatures or disarms its power. Altering the setting of the beautiful (defined as Marcuse does), conversely, makes the liberating quality of the beautiful apparent.

The power of Marcuse's definition of beauty lies in its association with "mind" rather than with "soul." In the dominant aesthetic of our culture beauty is transcendent, reaching us through that bourgeois organ of perception, the soul, that functions through a passive acceptance of reality, through "disinterestedness." Though beauty is separate from reality, the former needs the latter in order to remain stable. In this sense beauty acts to keep one fundamentally inert, or, more precisely, to keep eros on the periphery. For Marcuse beauty is opposed to reality but is not transcendent; instead it belongs to the pleasure principle, so that its opposition to reality is active and challenging and "nonrepressive." Rather than canceling out "mind," beauty requires it: critical thinking is activated in the presence of the beautiful and is experienced as pleasure.

All of this is, of course, very abstract. It is difficult to feel beauty as palpable, to locate it in one's experience of, say, poetry. More precisely, how does one know the presence of the two different kinds of beauty; how does one describe "desire" and the erotic in poetry and how do they reach us as conscious readers? I find it helpful to discuss Romanticism, particularly Romantic poetry, as dramatizing in our culture the competing drives toward consolation and critical consciousness, toward the beautiful as transcendence and the beautiful as erotic pleasure and desire. Romantic poetry often represents this competition. Although I began this study and will conclude it concerned primarily about poetry, I have come to believe that the representations of desire found in fiction and the essay are deeply relevant to my subject. The genre of poetry, in fact, must be considered a "position" in the competition about beauty. One question I will ask in this book is: why did poetry shoulder some of the most intense and complex representations of experience in the art of the Romantic period, taking over the position previously held by the novel?

I will try to answer this question in terms of the fate of beauty in modern culture. In Burke the beautiful is separated from the sublime, such that the beautiful becomes identified with the idyllic, the domestic, the social, the distant, the serene, a masculine view of femininity. Sublimity is associated with excitement and danger, with a simultaneous yielding to experience and control over it. But Plato (who may have the last, as well as the first, word on the subject of beauty) proposes a model of the experience of the beautiful which nearly encompasses *both* of Burke's two categories. By insisting upon the distinction between the sublime and the beautiful, Burke reinforces the separation of the beautiful from erotic turbulence and mental and aesthetic risk. If that turbulance belongs solely to the experience of the sublime, then it (turbulence or risk) refers to and has its being solely in the individual and her self-preservation, her self-enhancement. Beauty is a figure for happiness. When it becomes charged with an erotic consciousness, either beauty can be perceived as antithetical to its own vision of coherence and control, or it can be viewed as a form of itself challenging the current social and economic configuration.

In the Enlightenment and post-Enlightenment periods representations of erotic passion and desire are usually signs of a subversive social consciousness and energy. The lyric poems from the mid-eighteenth century on (in England)—with their escapist, ahistorical, anti-urban tendencies; with their focus on the meditative, solitary voice often immersed in the melancholy lake of past innocence; with their prevalent notion, in poets like Akenside and Collins, that poetry should provide for the "health" (consoling, integrating) of the privileged reader—conform to a beauty emptied of erotic passion. *Romantic poetry struggles, to greater and lesser degrees, to return representations of erotic desire, at times to force them, into the presence of beauty.*

Roland Barthes, in his essay "Diderot, Brecht, Eisenstein," discusses the social implications of the "scene" or "tableau" in Brecht's aesthetics of the theater (found previously in Diderot's aesthetics of painting as well):

> In order to tell a story, the painter possesses only one moment: the one he will immobilize on the canvas; hence, he must choose this moment well, affording it in advance the greatest possible yield of meaning and of pleasure: necessarily total, this moment will be artificial (unreal: this is not a realist art), it will be a hieroglyph in which can be read at a glance (in a single apprehension, if we turn to the theater, to the cinema) the present, the past, and the future, i.e., the historical meaning of the represented gesture.
>
> Brecht indicated clearly that in the epic theater (which proceeds by successive tableaux) the entire burden of meaning and of pleasure is conveyed by each scene, not by the whole; on the level of the play, no development, no ripening; an ideal meaning, of course (on the level of each scene, each tableau), but no *final* meaning, nothing but projections, each of which possesses a sufficient demonstrative power.[11]

Without the "gesture" the scene conveys a consoling sufficiency, or a consoling insufficiency in so far as it belongs to a developmental scheme in which case the scene exists only to be realized later on. The scene itself incurs no excitement, no particularly vital mental activity. With the gesture, says Barthes, we observe and participate in scene after scene in a state of "continual jubilation" of mental excitement because the scene becomes a story, in itself, of the fundamental conflictual elements of the society.

Marcuse associates a similar "gratification" with a beauty composed of, produced by, such conflictual elements:

> the work of art is beautiful to the degree to which it opposes its own order to that of reality—its non-repressive order where even the curse is still spoken in the name of Eros. It appears in the brief moments of fulfillment, tranquility—in the "beautiful moment" which arrests

the incessant dynamic and disorder, the constant need to do all that which has to be done in order to continue living.[12]

I do not believe that Marcuse means simply that beauty is a form of escape, an idyll in the midst of reality. The nonrepressive order ought to be the representation of the opposition between two visions (as in Blake's *Songs of Innocence and Experience: Shewing the Two Contrary States of the Human Soul*). Partly, then, this beauty-as-fundamental-conflict resides in the object of art; partly it resides, and is completed, in the experience of the observer/ reader who refuses to suppress one side of the conflict for the sake of consolation in the dominance of the other.

A musing by Bertolt Brecht in a 1940 diary entry written during the Battle of Britain focuses the problem of the bourgeois idyll of art: is it an escape or a vision of something better than current fascism? Wonderfully and surprisingly Brecht is meditating on Wordsworth:

> I skimmed a small volume of Wordsworth's poems in Arnold's edition. Came on "She was a phantom of delight" and reflected on this now remote work and on the dangers involved in laying down the law. Even such labels as "petty-bourgeois idyll" are hazardous. There are indeed some petty-bourgeois tendencies which are directed towards the perpetuation and consolidation of the petty-bourgeoisie as a class, but within the petty-bourgeoisie there are also other kinds of tendencies that conflict with those. The individual petty-bourgeois currently patrolling the English countryside equipped with a shotgun and a Molotov cocktail (as used against tanks in the Spanish Civil War, so a general assured us on the radio), has up to a point legitimate enough grounds for blaming his Wordsworths; yet it is just in dehumanised situations like these that
>
> > A lovely Apparition, sent
> > To be a moment's ornament
>
> helps to conjure up other situations less unworthy of the human race. Certainly ours is a time when the poem no longer serves "to haunt, to startle, to waylay."[13]

Here the conflict resides in the observer Brecht. Prepared to label the poem as hopelessly reinforcing of bourgeois ideology and, eventually, fascism, he admits to an element of human "worth" in these lines, of something not simply uplifting but potentially liberating. Presumably he finds in this bourgeois poem an emphasis on a principle other than that of power. He imagines a whole class of such poems, and points to a line in which the sameness of modern experience, the uniformity (as Wordsworth says in the *Preface to the Lyrical Ballads*) of life in cities is broken by an erotic vision, the "shock" that lifts the viewer out of a petty-bourgeois reverie to set him forward into the intense, fantastic consciousness of love. This is the better "tendency" that conflicts, for Brecht, with the current fascism.

But clearly this conflict does, in fact, reside in the poem itself: if it is fundamentally a poem of the bourgeoisie, written by a poet like Wordsworth, the poem nonetheless contains within it that better tendency. Is it mere coincidence that Brecht's eye catches the very lines that mark for the speaker his own shock of erotic awakening, the moment in which experience is suddenly enlivened, in which fantasy opens and the risk of love begins? This is the moment upon which many eighteenth-century novels of passion-love turn, the moment that sets in motion the blighted heroism of the lover and that rocks the domestic stability organizing modern society.

> She was a Phantom of delight
> When first she gleamed upon my sight;
> A lovely Apparition, sent
> To be a moment's ornament;
> Her eyes as stars of Twilight fair;
> Like Twilight's, too, her dusky hair;
> But all things else about her drawn
> From May-time and the cheerful Dawn;
> A dancing Shape, an Image gay,
> To haunt, to startle, and way-lay.
>
> I saw her upon nearer view,
> A Spirit, yet a Woman too!
> Her household motions light and free,
> And steps of virgin-liberty;
> A countenance in which did meet
> Sweet records, promises as sweet;
> A Creature not too bright or good
> For human nature's daily food;
> For transient sorrows, simple wiles,
> Praise, blame, love, kisses, tears, and smiles.

> And now I see with eye serene
> The very pulse of the machine;
> A Being breathing thoughtful breath,
> A Traveller between life and death;
> Endurance, foresight, strength, and skill;
> A perfect Woman, nobly planned,
> To warn, to comfort, and command;
> And yet a Spirit still, and bright
> With something of angelic light.

Before reading Brecht's casual note on the poem, I was prepared to argue that the opening stanza of passion exists only in order to dissolve before the more compelling power of domestic liberty (constrained, virginal) and the final resting place of angelic, mentalized spirit ("A Being breathing thoughtful breath"). But Wordsworth's canceling and, to him, transcendence of the moment of disorientation and illumination did not phase the German Marxist poet of the people; Brecht was startled, haunted, and waylaid by the representation of that which startled the poet-lover. This suggests to me that what Wordsworth planned as an account of a single-minded evolution of consciousness can be read as a scene of fundamental conflict: the moment of passion versus its domestication and spiritualization.

What is the fate of beauty in this conflict? In the opening stanza the risk of the beautiful and the risk of love are about the same. Whereas in the subsequent stanzas these risks decline into the evolving, strengthening subjectivity of the poet and into the sturdy household, transcended objectivity of the female, here they lie in the moment of dispersal of social and individualized realities into the haunted space of apparition and image. By the end of the poem the lover (if he can still be called that) dwells in serene disinterestedness; his gaze presumably controls his household as well as it obviously has diminished his passions. The woman breathing full of thought presumably does not breathe with desire; from the rest of the last stanza, it is clear that her "thought" exists for her benign, admonitory virtues in the family. Desire in the woman, as well as for him, becomes a forlorn possibility. "Sight" marks the firm, complete knowledge of the woman, but at the beginning "sight" produced the confusion of the senses, the occasion for desire, the possibility for change. Beauty, therefore, is associated with a disruption that could have defined the poem. However, the later stanzas associate beauty with continuity, the autobiography of the poet's gaze ("I saw her upon nearer view," "And now I see with eye serene . . ."). As Allen Grossman has said of Hart Crane, in a formulation that could apply generally to the "greater Romantic lyric": "desire has given way to the criteria of civility." [14]

The reader, I believe, is free to follow the narrator-poet and find beauty in the serene stability of domestic spirituality, or else find it in the coherence of the conflict between the stability of the end and the instability of the beginning. In the latter way a picture emerges of the contradictions in Wordsworth's society; instead of producing sheer wonderment, beauty allows for a conscious, and therefore troubling pleasure.

With Keats and Shelley, the next generation of the Romantics, beauty becomes even more intensely identified with the erotic; often the poet seems to wish to recover an erotic passion that an earlier (Wordsworthian) poet wished to silence or disarm. The intensity reaches a fever pitch in Keats's poems to his beloved Fanny Brawne where, in one case, the metaphor of a "Bright star" must sustain the ideal of serene disinterestedness and erotic passion. Whereas in "She Was a Phantom of Delight" the poet could try to dissolve and transcend the erotic passion of first encounter dialectically over time, Keats refuses to allow desire to be separated from any spiritualized resolution, so that the hunger for that resolution must be compressed into the space of desire itself.

> Bright star, would I were stedfast as thou art—
>   Not in lone splendour hung aloft the night
> And watching, with eternal lids apart,
>   Like nature's patient, sleepless Eremite,
> The moving waters at their priestlike task
>   Of pure ablution round earth's human shores,
> Or gazing on the new soft-fallen mask
>   Of snow upon the mountains and the moors—
> No—yet still stedfast, still unchangeable,
>   Pillow'd upon my fair love's ripening breast,
> To feel for ever its soft fall and swell,
>   Awake for ever in a sweet unrest,
> Still, still to hear her tender-taken breath,
> And so live ever—or else swoon to death.

How is beauty manifest in "Bright Star," in contrast to "She Was a Phantom of Delight"?

Although there is a subjectivity in this poem, it does not appear as an autobiographical one; nor does it focus attention upon itself. Instead it dwindles before its own longings and fantasies, by which a field of desire is implied where beauty resides. Beauty neither transcends desire nor resides in a protracted individual subjectivity.

The poem sustains an opposition between disinterestedness and engagement, between the sense of sight and the sense of touch, between perspective and intimacy, between a chaste beauty and an erotic one. Even though the syntax of the poem gives preference to the second of each of these pairs, the poetic empathy in the first part (the octave) renders such preference equivocal and permanently unresolvable.

The intensity of the poetic language—imagery, alliteration, and assonance—focuses attention on language itself, away from experience. The erotic elements of beauty presume this lifting of language from its experiential base.

Leopardi said of "works of genius" that "they always serve as a consolation, rekindling enthusiasm, and though speaking of and portraying nothing but death, restore to [a great soul], at least for awhile, the life that it had lost." [15] A poem like "Bright Star," however, offers more than consolation; its beauty lies not in its sheer articulation of misery but rather in the challenge it poses, within its borders, to two completely conflicting desires and their consequences. In this state I cannot say with Keats on another occasion that beauty "overcomes all other considerations," that it ends in "speculation," because there is not that final resting place in wonderment. And yet it would be imprecise to suggest that wonderment does not play a part in the experience of this conflict-laden version of beauty. Can we call mystical what happens when the conflict of ideas comes under the influence of aesthetic experience? While we are entering into Keats's idealist versus materialist antithesis, which throws us back into our individuality, do we not also feel that link to all the other readers of this poem, one of the characteristics of beauty? A feeling of connectedness to a community of readers, to—more extravagantly—a universal readership, is hard to measure; but the experience of reading "Bright Star" in the manner just described is hardly isolating. Recall that from the idealist, bourgeois perspective beauty ought to touch the "soul," to reach into the desire-free and reality-free space of self- and class-affirmation. In the proposed readings of both Wordsworth's and Keats's poems, "mind," rather than "soul," is active and receives not consolation but gratification. The conflictual elements in the poems stimulate in the mind the pleasure of conscious conflict. This particular pleasure is reinforced by the hunger of the reader for consolation, combined with a refusal to dwell in that complacent state; illusion and reality can both be valued here.

And so can hope. Stendhal's definition of beauty controverts the idealist one: "une promesse de bonheur." Benjamin adds: "our image of happiness is indissolubly bound up with the image of redemption." Although this may create terrible, unrealizable longings, it also releases a utilizable energy, one inseparable from a critical consciousness: if happiness—in the beautiful— exists "out there," what conditions in the present, both within myself and without, cry out for transformation?

I have suggested that the peculiar conflict available in Romantic poetry is often stimulated by the representations of erotic passion and desire that threaten the pure serene of ideal beauty in the Romantic lyric. These representations appear throughout the Romantic period without an affinity for any particular genre. The novel, the poem, and the essay all confirm the potentially unsettling force of erotic passion and desire.

What I wish to convey in the rest of this book is precisely what is unsettling and how it is so. When I began to dwell amidst the lively confusion of this problem, I wrote in a manner designed to avoid oversimplifying the troubling experience of reading Romantic literature from the perspective I have described. It seemed that the allures and limitations of beauty, the tempting disruptions created by representations of desire in literature, the conflicts between spirituality in Romantic literature and the demystifications of social critique, belonged equally to the writers and to myself—or ourselves as modern readers. The words of Schiller and Adorno seem to me now, as then, to organize a problem also belonging to the Romantics and ourselves, that of disinterested observation versus engagement:

> [The Modern Artist] will indeed take his subject matter from the present age, but his form he will borrow from a nobler time—nay, from beyond all time, from the absolute unchangeable unity of his being.[16]

> the spontaneous movement of the object can be followed only by someone who is not engulfed by it.[17]

I am trying, in the following pages, to present the drama of an observer of a cultural situation, Western Romanticism, as I am at once drawn to the images of the beautiful and wary of them. As Schiller and Adorno imply, critical distance—when one engages the beautiful—is problematical. (Adorno, in his difficult essay, best demonstrates the problem of distance: where is that uncontaminated place? I am produced by and composed of that from which I wish to separate myself. My terms are its terms.) I have tried to make the *form* of my inquiry—short, speculative essays dominated by insight rather than by extended scholarly argument—part of the distance. Also part of the critical observations: not for egotistical reasons, but as representative of the kind of reader who slowly wakes up from an uncritical idealism in his embrace of Romantic vision and poetic language, have I charted in these pages my urgent intellectual and emotional stumblings from a celebration of Romantic essentialism to its critique. (Essentialism, in this case, refers to a preference for and indications of the principle of unity in aesthetic objects and the principle of an ahistorical essential "self," unpersuaded and unmodified by the environment but perceived as singularly available to destruction by society and social ambition and erotic desire.) The spirit of this reorganization involves not so much a skepticism about essentialist preferences as a wonderment in the face of the "low breathings" of the Romantic undersongs and countersongs of passion, an excitement over the discovery that Romanticism, or more precisely the cultural tradition that has by and large carried Romanticism to us over the past two hundred years, has repressed or (as Foucault might say) disarmed the revolutionary and subversive intention and effect of much of the Romantic representation of erotic passion. I have tried to write in a way that points precisely to the words, the texts, the figures in Romanticism that have been for me the sites of the recovery of the power of Romantic passion. How accurately, I have asked myself for this book, can I describe the vicissitudes of my response to the beautiful, the beautiful as it impinges on and partakes of the passionate and the transformative, in Romantic literature? Can I pinpoint some moments in these works when the dual nature (spiritual and critical) of my response to the beautiful leaps forth?

(At times the reader may perceive that I place beauty in opposition to a corrupt culture but do not make it undermining of that culture. In developing a more energetic response to the beautiful, however, one necessarily engages it at more and less retrograde levels. Consolation, after all, is the primary way of experiencing beauty in our society.)

The Romantics, unfailingly associated with the repression of history, are not generally associated with the repression or disarming of erotic passion.

I find that in Romanticism history and eros challenge and threaten the complacency of authors (with their idyllic versions of the beautiful) in connected ways. I have come to believe that a proper feminist reassessment of Romantic literature must engage the representation of passion and erotic fantasy, its predictable and subsequent suppression, the disarming of its destabilizing potential. More specifically, that reassessment ought to mark those writers for whom and those occasions when passion and fantasy are and are not suppressed and disarmed. Indeed, a characteristic difference between the early and later generations of English Romantic male writers may lie in their literary/political convictions about passion and fantasy.

The notes that follow chart moments of an intellectual and spiritual journey I have taken (and continue to take) along the path made by Romantic literary artifacts and by the cultural ambivalences that have brought Romanticism to the present day. The following observations will take the reader not only along the same path of representations of passion and desire but also through discussions of the Romantic autobiographical impulse and of the Romantic, Coleridgean imagination as each is threatened and organized by the problem (as it is perceived) of desire. Finally, behind these discussions is the question: what do representations of passion and desire do to the fate of beauty?

[2]

The Sentiment of

Existence—I

When, in book VI of the *Aeneid*, the shade of Dido vanishes into the shadowy arms of her shade-husband Sychaeus before the pleas of her bewildered, burdened lover/murderer Aeneas, Virgil has caught the harshness of the premodern world toward the need of the individual for tender love. Dante later invites us to that need when his Virgil picks up the hero, *as a mother picks up her child,* in order to advance him on the career of his meaningful journey.

It is not until Rousseau envisions a "sentiment of existence" that the principle of tender, protective pleasure enters the Western consciousness never to leave it.[1] At this moment Romanticism is born.

With hindsight I can say that Virgil noted this elemental pleasure by its absence, its denials, and the presence of Aeneas' harsh grief. Who, after all, can live—unmodified and uncompromised—without such pleasure? Romanticism, in Rousseau, Goethe, and Wordsworth, knew that the infant's pleasure with its parent needs many reinvestments and recommitments at later moments in life.

The ancient world is at least as harsh with that other pleasure, the pleasure of eroticism. The passion produced toward and out of eroticism becomes tragedy in the *Aeneid*, as with Dido and Aeneas, or it becomes harshly displaced onto the irrational mania for warfare. The women of the *Aeneid* send their cries of passion into the empty air or into destruction of self and others. When it returns in Romanticism—as in Keats, Shelley, Byron, and Hazlitt—passion couples the personal urgency with a social one: sexual passion and social criticism tend to join their energies. So there is hope in this passion, just as there is hope in the "sentiment of existence," but the two diverge as I picture them: one risking the integrity of the self for realities (personal and social) beyond the self, the other risking the loss of the world for the final integrity of self. If I tend, conventionally, to think of passion and the fantasies of passion as a form of self-absorption, I extend myself to believe that the opposite is true: passion exists only in the presence of the world and the consciousness of the world.

Besides, even the infant—as observers from Augustine on know—quickly learns other, less tender, pleasures of the body and pleasures of desire.

The Sentiment of
Existence—II

Rousseau lying in his rowboat on the Lake of Bienne becomes an integer.[1] He feels like God, like the infant rocked and nursed by its mother. He knows the sentiment of existence, an elemental, nearly "physiological" sentiment, the original feeling, the feeling of life.

Life produces in the human animal a sentiment, a limited but certain consciousness of well-being, perhaps what Wordsworth later calls the "grand elementary principle of pleasure."[2] Like Rousseau, Wordsworth describes the "sentiment of Being" as oceanic feeling: "I, at this time / Saw blessings spread around me like a sea" (*1805 Prelude*, II, 413–14). Should not all our lives be founded on such a self-confirming sentiment and be protected and molded by it?

These two Romantics formulate a condition of pure existence; then they humanize it with what they consider the purest of responses: feeling. Rousseau asserts the foreignness of thought to this elemental condition. Thought is an antagonist, a pollution of existential consciousness. Without naming it, Wordsworth clearly associates the experience of beauty with this transcendence of thought:

> I was only then
> Contented when with bliss ineffable
> I felt the sentiment of Being spread
> O'er all that moves, and all that seemeth still,
> O'er all, that, lost beyond the reach of thought
> And human knowledge, to the human eye
> Invisible, yet liveth to the heart,
> O'er all that leaps, and runs, and shouts, and sings,
> Or beats the gladsome air, o'er all that glides
> Beneath the wave, yea, in the wave itself
> And mighty depth of waters.
>
> (II, 418–28)

A deception wraps itself around the rhetoric of Rousseau's sentiment of existence: it lives in alienation and downright hostility. Rousseau had recently written *Emile* and *The Social Contract*, both received in hatred and violence by the French and Swiss authorities; and in Switzerland he wears provocative, outlandish Armenian garb. People throw rocks at his window. The Swiss police imprison him on the Isle of St. Pierre, where he claims his elemental happiness. He claims to wish that they would imprison him here for life, or, if they like, imprison him in the Bastille.

The Reveries of the Solitary Walker propose a set of conditions in which the social emotions vanish. Rousseau wants to decathect the world, to abandon all fantasy.

Fantasy presumes the consciousness of other vital human subjects. This wish to abandon fantasy, so common in Romanticism, marks the point at which I must invoke, nearly simultaneously, psychological and historical criticism. For it is the person's wish, in his assumed solitude, but at the same time it is the Romantic victory over malevolent society; it is not a politically radical solution since many avowed radicals of the period approaching the French Revolution and the Revolution itself would consider the formulation of the sentiment of existence a utopian construct leading them far from the necessary field of action.

Rousseau's wish, in fact, *is* a fantasy—a fantasy of total domination fired by the abandoned infant's rage.

[4]

The Sentiment of Existence and

the Shock from Nature

According to Freud, and in a more literary setting Benjamin, the person experiences the world outside himself through shocks and disruptions of an essential tranquility of nonconsciousness. In Wordsworth the shock is fundamentally welcoming and confirming. Wandering lonely as a cloud, he opens into consciousness through the crowd or host of daffodils. Later in the nineteenth century the otherness is more noxious—and earlier in Rousseau. Ideally the resistance to the world is partial, availing the self of the energy and the news of difference, but avoiding a revolution or anarchy of self. Self and world alienate each other in consciousness. Rousseau and Wordsworth continually revert to the self's luxurious complacency before the world, and Schiller to the "filled infinity" [1] of the mind as possibility before intrusive, invasive "reality" annihilates or severely limits possibility. In Baudelaire ("A une passante") the shock is in the love object, or rather the man's feelings are shocked by the sight of the heavenly woman in the crowd. [2] (Note that in "a crowd, a host of daffodils" Wordsworth's "crowd" metaphorizes or converts society into flowers, this naturalization being a favorite trick of Romantic ideology. Similarly with "host" the poet confers upon the urban reference, "crowd," a religious association.)

Rousseau on a *promenade* was reviewing his life, in grateful complacency, as an orderly sequence of innocent and loving gestures, when a Great Dane smashed him to the pavement in an unchecked onrush of animal violence. Nature in its pre-idyllic manifestation—eruptive, volcanic—demolished the precious human scaffolding of unconcern. What remained, or emerged, from this violation was . . . the sentiment of existence, the consciousness of being without reference or prop or definition by the outside—a "delicious" sentiment, a "wonderful calm," "nothing to compare with it in all the pleasures that stir our lives." [3]

The sentiment of existence cannot permeate daily life. Only language notes it after the fact, further to alienate it from experience and therefore to alienate the self-in-experience from this now transcending desire.

At one point in the passage Rousseau describes the injuries and disfigurements suffered by his body with more anatomical specificity than anyone since Homer described the penetration of the spear or sword into the body of a newly inert heroic consciousness. For Homer no sentiment of existence follows. He anticipates even more than Rousseau Rousseau's ambivalent admirer William Hazlitt, who reports on a boxing match. Here is the climax:

> Neate just then made a tremendous lunge at him, and hit him full in the face. It was doubtful whether he would fall backwards or forwards; he hung suspended for a second or two, and then fell back, throwing his hands in the air, and with his face lifted up to the sky. I never saw any thing more terrific than his aspect just before he fell. All traces of life, of natural expression, were gone from him. His face was like a human skull, a death's head, spouting blood. The eyes were filled with blood, the nose streamed with blood, the mouth gaped blood. He was not like an actual man, but like a preternatural, spectral appearance, or like one of the figures in Dante's *Inferno*. Yet he fought on after this for several rounds, still striking the first desperate blow, and Neate standing on the defensive, and using the same cautious guard to the last, as if he had still all his work to do. . . .[4]

Instead of the sentiment of existence, Hazlitt raises the class consciousness of his reader: instead of transcendence and rapturous calm there is the shiver of aristocratic confidence (i.e., literary language) breaking against lower-class muscle.

I recall my own shock, upon first reading this passage, at discovering that Rousseau's and Wordsworth's solution to these momentous intrusions might be considered an instance of withdrawal (the turtle shrinking into its shell) and self-protection, that what appeared as transcendence might not be a true expansion of self, that not all explosive encounters may feel like an intrusion.

[5]

The Romantic Poet

as Orestes

The Romantic theorist of that most Romantic of genres, the idyll, Friedrich Schiller, envisions the contemporary poet growing into and performing in a purgatorial violence:

> No doubt the artist is the child of his time; but woe to him if he is also its disciple, or even its favourite. Let some beneficent deity snatch the infant betimes from his mother's breast, let it nourish him with the milk of a better age and suffer him to grow up to full maturity beneath the distant skies of Greece. Then when he has become a man, let him return to his century as an alien figure; but not in order to gladden it by his appearance, rather, terrible like Agamemnon's son, to cleanse it. He will indeed take his subject matter from the present age, but his form he will borrow from a nobler time—nay, from beyond all time, from the absolute unchangeable unity of his being. Here, from the pure aether of his daemonic nature, flows forth the wellspring of Beauty, untainted by the corruption of the generations and ages which wallow in the dark eddies below it.[1]

In the midst of this idealist construction of artistic efficacy, in the midst of a view of an artist detached from prejudices and commitments of the moment, lies an association to Orestes, a hardly disinterested figure, doing violence to his mother because the latter did violence to him by killing his father. The real Orestes was beset by the Furies who instilled in him the maddened, inflamed consciousness of the socially oppressed.

By means of this comparison, Schiller's artist also contains within him a potentially revolutionary consciousness and vision. The artist will be alienated from social corruption and instinctual rage by his education in innocence; he will become violent through his nurturance in the pure serene of beauty. Beauty will become the vision of social difference and thus will be revolutionary. Orestes, moreover, affirmed the affiliative relationship with his sister Electra, a relationship that contradicts the power struggles and blindnesses and self-interestedness of the filiative connections to parents.

The affiliative vision, of course, becomes central to the Romantic revolutionary consciousness.

Yet Schiller's choice of comparison—the modern artist as Orestes—points out the Romantic ambivalence toward the artist's function: in Aeschylus Orestes' violent act culminated not in revolution and change and in the emergence of a new order but in the reinforcement of the old patriarchy and a mollifying of the dissatisfactions of the oppressed. The idyllic and beautiful and the violent do not appear to oppose or cancel out each other; violence ought to cleanse or purge but not necessarily stimulate a new consciousness, a new society. Is the purging of corruption through artistic beauty really, then, a purging at all? Or is it in fact a consolation?

Schiller's association to the Orestes story raises a question about the politics of Romantic form: should we listen to the middle of the story, which often contains the seeds of social and psychological destabilization, or to the end of the story, in which those seeds dry up to preserve effectually the old order?

[6]

Schiller: Beauty and Desire

"Man, um jenes politische Problem in der Erfahrung zu loesen, durch das aesthetische den Weg nehmen muss, weil es die Schoenheit ist, durch welche man zu der Freiheit wandert." [1] (In order to solve that political problem in practice, one must take the path of the aesthetic since it is beauty through which one wanders to freedom.)

Near the beginning of *On the Aesthetic Education of Man* (first published in 1795), Schiller instructs us to believe that the impulse for his idealist aesthetics originated in the call for freedom in the French Revolution and, as with the English Romantics, in the muting of that call by the Reign of Terror. But it quickly emerges that "freedom" means specifically and immediately not "civic freedom" but rather a disinterested, contemplative freedom—linked vaguely to a vision of transformed community. How perfect, therefore, that Schiller imagines the exchange of beauty for freedom as a wandering journey. A staple of German poetry from Goethe and Eichendorff to Hesse, the wanderer encounters the (usually natural) world in his solitude and from a distance that insures that his possible response to the social will have been diffused in the beautiful, which often stands in for a longing for home. Late in the *Aesthetic Education*, Schiller underscores the journey motif by observing that we "step" (*treten*) with beauty into the world of ideas and "pass" (*uebergehen*) from beauty to truth.

There is something chaste, even ascetic, in this journey. Although we live in the midst of our drives (*Trieb*)—sense, form, and play—our journey takes us past drive and desire to contemplation and disinterestedness; it is beauty that guides us past desire, that "tempers" it. But only in the most liberal of cultures can we (men) achieve the greatest of aesthetic experiences—to "perceive in [living feminine beauty] itself only pure appearance . . . [and] to dispense with life in the appearance." [2] In the presence of a beautiful woman we face the greatest challenge, to know beauty without experiencing, knowing desire; by subduing desire.

Rousseau's Ambivalence about Passion

Rousseau's fear of adolescent and adult passion permeates almost all of his later work. In one way he simply updates the Western fear of passion, the recognition of its inevitability and its power, from the earliest times. But he sets in motion the terms and focus of much Romantic psychopolitical debate in literature.

Passion, he says, is natural, and yet some passions are more "natural" than others. Actually there is only one good natural passion: "The origin of our passions, the root and spring of all the rest, the only one which is born with man, which never leaves him as long as he lives, is self-love. . . ." [1] This is the principle of self-preservation, begun in infancy and often lost to view as life proceeds. Adolescence is the dangerous time for the passions: "As the roaring of the waves precedes the tempest, so the murmur of rising passions announces this tumultuous change; a suppressed excitement warns us of the approaching danger." [2] "External influences" produce the new passions and are completely harmful. The adolescent is becoming a social and sexual being, living not in the relatively inconsequential shelter of family but probing the larger, more reactive world. The adolescent, largely through the erotic energy of body and mind, *has an effect*. In the literature of Goethe, Schiller, Blake, and Wordsworth, the adolescent may provide the impetus, the indignation, the intelligence, and the physical energy, for revolution. Rousseau dedicates his intelligence in *Emile* to the dissipation of all this adolescent passion into the inconsequential; he wants his young man's drives to reinforce a new idyllic, patriarchal order.

Rousseau's *amour de soi* is one important place where "passion" or desire and "pleasure" blur. Passion gets lost in the "at-homeness" of pleasure.

> Let the winged Fancy roam;
> Pleasure never is at home.

Keats, somewhat mournfully, separates them (December 1818). But there is life in that separation as Fancy roams on wing. Sexuality and freedom, eros as hope, soars. Will the new pleasure be as solitary as Rousseau's on the Lake of Bienne?

[8]

The Lively Pleasure

. . . if I could manage to confine myself to the lively pleasures the other affords me, without contaminating them, mortifying them by the anxiety which serves as their hinge? . . . and then, if I managed systematically to forget the zones of alarm which separate these moments of pleasure?
—Roland Barthes, *A Lover's Discourse*

On a journey Rousseau meets Madame de Larnage. There is mutual attraction though it emerges slowly through his reticence and his illness of vapors and a *polypus*. She persists in her attraction and finally reaches his burdened desire by embracing him. This leads to one of the rare moments of lovemaking in the *Confessions*:

> This delicious existence lasted three or four days during which I grew drunk upon the sweetest of pleasures. They were pure and sharp and without any alloy of pain; and they were the first and the last I have ever savoured in that way. . . . If what I felt for her was not precisely love, it was at least so tender a return for the love she showed me, there was so hot a sensuality in our pleasures and so sweet an intimacy in our talk, that it had all the charm of passion without that delirium which turns the head and makes enjoyment impossible.[1]

I recall the congratulatory mood with which, upon first arriving at this nearly halfway point in the *Confessions*, I greeted Rousseau's triumph in sexual pleasure! What a victory over his inhibitions! What an affirmation of his fundamental delight in the body and mastery of intimate expression! But I think this is how Rousseau wants me to respond; the expert manipulation of the reader in this book does not flag even at this pitch of self-abandon. As sexual love, in this passage, over time becomes apparently to me an *ideology* of sexual love, I detect a familiar pattern of Rousseauian construction around the moment of naturalness and spontaneity.

This intensity flourishes, significantly, in a moment, a three-day island of pleasure. Separated from his familiar acquaintances, from his commitments, he enters into a kind of *amor ignotus*. In part II of the *Confessions* anonymity is no longer possible. Rousseau would like to cultivate a pleasurable isolation, but neither society nor his own hunger for social attachment and involvement will grant him that bliss of solitude. The social emotions, *amour propre,* that tie him masochistically to the world of power rule out sexual love.

I look at Rousseau's memory of love ("not precisely love") with Mme. de Larnage as a private experience encompassing a range of sensations, from hot to sweet, from sensuality to tenderness and charm, a mixture of elements and free from pain, and think: what fullness in his experience! how complete is his love! and yet, knowing Rousseau, I wonder if the tenderness mitigates the heat in the sense of preventing the fulfillment of love, if in this representation of sexual pleasure the opposites in experience reinforce the isolation of the moment from the rest of life, make the moment transcendent in the sense of "above" experience. The moment seems to belong to the sentiment of existence, created to keep out the social emotions and consequences and to avoid the "delirium" of passion and fantasy that weds love to the social identity.

Rousseau may say that the moment of sexual love was memorably unique for him and unique partly because it was without consequence. Looking past his own rhetoric, however, I can see consequences. He plans to meet Mme. de Larnage later on but does not. He then returns to Mamma, Mme. de Warens, with whom he has been living in sad ambiguity as loverson, to discover that another lover has replaced him. This dissolves the ambiguity (an ambiguity that could have similarly developed with Mme. de Larnage), and he from then on becomes in her presence "pure child." He had cultivated this purity—very erotic for a child—and dependency with Mme. de Larnage. Only when she seduced him did he feel like a man, did love become so pleasurable, was its transferability to new situations utterly impossible.

Rousseau does not encourage, agonize over, the passions of love. He does not suffer from temptation as much as he cuts temptation out at the root. This violence done to the fantasy life is undone by the progressive writers about erotic passion: e.g., Goethe, Blake, Hazlitt, Keats, Shelley, and above all Stendhal in *De l'amour.* When he brings passion and erotic fantasies into the story of love, the Romantic writer insists that love belongs to the social person, that the intense feelings of desire for the beloved may challenge the stability of a domestic system that fears intense feelings.

For the Romantic writer such erotic intensity therefore has a politically subversive overtone.

But who would wish to deny Rousseau his lively pleasure, remembered fondly, possessively into his gouty old age?

[9]

"The Grand Elementary
Principle of Pleasure"

For years I believed that Lionel Trilling was right to identify Words-worth's "pleasure" with Freud's "drive," something tied to instinct, an inherent, biological push toward resolution.[1] It was appealing to imagine that Wordsworth, unpredictably, respected the drives, something beneath consciousness and often expressed through fantasy, and found them worthy of representation in his poetry and worthy of a central place in his manifesto on poetry.

Now, somewhat reluctantly, I want to give up that equation of Words-worthian pleasure and Freudian drive; I see this Romantic poet's pleasure as a wish for an idyll of the drive. In that wish I recognize the presence and the power of the instinctual life but refuse to accede to its destabilizing potential. But Wordsworth—in contrast to, for example, Blake or Hazlitt or at times Keats and Byron, who probe relentlessly the connection between the drive and the experience of pleasure—seems far less a Freudian poet and much more a Rousseauian one. His "pleasure" accords more with the "sentiment of existence," "elementary" or "essential" not because it belongs to the id more than to the ego but because it resides in extrasocial purity. The purpose of poetry is to give pleasure to the reader by touching upon his "humanity," his self divested of role, divested of power, divested of a fantasy, divested of sensuality. Wordsworth's pleasure would dominate in the idyllic patriarchal setting of *Emile*.

Why did Trilling wish to turn Wordsworth into a Freudian poet? Trilling's "drive," however, is strangely immobile. "Drive" does not foster disturbance or change or even desire but rather stands like a rock or anchor against the perceived waywardness of mind and passion. Yet there is a Romantic origin for this "rock-like in endurance" character, in Schiller, whose tragic heroes and heroines ascend to tragedy through a prodigious passivity of *endurance,* a remarkable resistance to passional and social presence. Again, it is the idealist vision of transcendence that imagines this rocklike quality. Trilling, by interpreting "pleasure" romantically, is interpreting Freud conservatively. But it raises the question: how far is Rous-

seau, lapped by the gentle waves of his lake, from Wordsworth's Happy
Warrior:

> More skilful in self-knowledge, even more pure,
> As tempted more; more able to endure,
> As more exposed to suffering and distress. . . .

[10]

Blake's Joseph and Mary

> I love my dear Joseph
> But he driveth me away from his presence. yet I hear
>   the voice of God
> In the voice of my Husband. tho he is angry for a
>   moment, he will not
> Utterly cast me away. if I were pure, never could I
>   taste the sweets
> Of the Forgiveness of Sins! if I were holy! I never
>   could behold the tears
> Of love! of him who loves me in the midst of his anger
>   in furnace of fire.[1]

In this amazing love scene from *Jerusalem*, the woman Mary interprets all the apparently negative passion of her angry/jealous husband (over the Virgin Birth) as expressions of love. Thus she does not need to cultivate love as a psychological idyll since there is nothing she needs to defend except faulty and restricted vision.

Indeed, purity and holiness, the condition of idyllic love, create the myopia of jealousy; the full and natural expression of sexual love grants wholeness to the lover and the beloved. Passion and fantasy are not "fond and wayward thoughts," as Wordsworth says, but that anger belonging to love. As Joseph recognizes in his anger the truth of Mary's song, she in turn "burst forth into a Song! she flowed like a River of / Many Streams in the arms of Joseph & gave forth her tears of joy / Like many waters. . . ." Neither lover needs to defend against sensations of pleasure, passions, and the fulfillment of love beyond the ego and the personal body.

Significantly, the woman—as in *Visions of the Daughters of Albion*—liberates passion and love into mutual pleasure. The singing river of love and the tears of joy become . . . the CREATION.

11

Two Passages from Joubert

We use for passions the stuff that has been given to us for happiness.

My soul lives in a place where the passions have passed by and where I have known them all.[1]

The point, I believe, is that a space and substance of human value resides beyond passion. We confuse passion with the promise of or hope for happiness, which is a thing of the spirit, the soul; indeed the identification of one's soul may coincide with the exclamation of happiness. The passions seem relevant for the recognition of both soul and happiness but only in a negative sense, in one's having defeated or surpassed them with one's knowledge of them. From the point of view of the still soul, they appear as the necessary epiphenomena of becoming.

In this quintessentially Romantic understanding, passion belongs to biology, just as adolescence does. Passion is only secondarily environmental in origin. That passion may be mobilized fundamentally to challenge a social situation, that happiness may reside in realizing in a society a vision of, as Dorothy Wordsworth says, "fairer worlds than this,"[2] is not considered.

12

"Bright Star" on the Lawn

I cannot discard the thought that my personal history with Romanticism—the farther back it goes, the better—contains some truth about the subject of this inquiry. Ultimately one's view of any subject, if it comes with conviction, does not so much appear full-blown at the moment of its expression, but digs deep into past voluntary and perhaps involuntary collisions of self with some version of the subject. "So feeling comes in aid of feeling. . . ."

I memorized my first Romantic poem, Keats's sonnet "Bright Star," [1] while mowing our lawn at, I believe, age thirteen. Carrying a pocketbook of Keats open to the page, I would read a line or two several times over and then repeat it many times as I mowed several rows of grass. This way the passionate sonnet about a then unknown feeling and involvement and precariousness worked itself word by word into me ("No—yet still steadfast, still unchangeable, Pillow'd upon my fair love's ripening breast"). The episode, when it comes back to me as it often does, returns in the color *green*—the bright, light green of grass in early summer, the color of the idyll. The poem gave off nothing but the most generous adolescent emotion, a full and infinite longing and pleasure-in-longing reinforced by the double pleasure evoked by Keats, of the sensuousness both of distant viewing and of the infinite closeness of the female body. The poem yielded no conflict of passion, but a potentially agonizing masculine fantasy of controlling solitude, sensuous love that one intensely imagines will go in the intensity of its coming.

In my green view of "Bright Star" passion was not a problem but a simple, welcoming solution to my vanishing preadolescence. I do not mean to elegize passion, Keats's sonnet, or adolescence but rather to reflect upon the origin of a personal identification with Romanticism, an identification that took years to modify and complicate. This was partly for personal resistances to change and consolations wrought from the idyllic strain in the Romantic worldview and poem, and partly from the pervasive critical tradition since the early nineteenth century that has confined the Romantic representation of passion to an early-adolescent exuberance implying little consequence.

[13]

Beauty and Anxiety

One lives so badly, because one always comes into the
present unfinished, unable, and distracted.[1]

This represents a Romantic view of the present as a locus of, an occasion
for, common, daily tragedy. Suppose instead one could simply breathe in
the midst of the unfinished, the unable, the distracted? What a relief! But
this would not be Romanticism.

One would also confront more palpably the presence of risk in our endeavors and desires. Rilke's insistence upon the possibility, if only rhetorical
possibility (which still gets under one's skin), of the finished, the able, the
focused all in the embrace of the present, decreases our consciousness of
relief and risk while it increases our anxiety, our distraction.

What would happen, in art, to the beautiful? Would it become more
modest? Would it become more disruptive? more erotic? How much of the
beautiful, under Romanticism, bears the dead weight of anxiety about the
present?

[14]

Return to the

Lake

of Bienne

Reading Blake compels me to reconsider Rousseau's *amour de soi* from a feminist vantage point. Rousseau in his rowboat on the Lake of Bienne seems to have finally escaped social reality; the fetters of social desire (*amour propre*), he claims, have withered away before the rhythmic rocking of the boat. He has retreated to, achieved, a condition of being, a place beyond politics. And yet, as he shows both in the *Confessions* and in the later *Reveries*, he is surrounded by the police, imprisoned in his island freedom. (The same could be said of his genre for his final work, reveries: he invokes a preconscious state to describe the mind in its condition of work, a state freed from amorous ties to the social and sexual world. All desire turns toward the self and toward the taste of the words his mind produces. But the *Reveries* surprisingly reveal, in place of a mind wandering lonely as a cloud, a very contentious consciousness, a battler with a maligning public. Their energy comes precisely from the defiant, argumentative position of the author.)

Rousseau lying supine in his boat, oars floating in the water by his side, suggests complete submission, complete vulnerability. Yet mentally he is free and strong. *He resists the penetration of an intrusive and pursuant society.* The reverie is a defiant form, a defiant state of mind. Perhaps it is in this light that one should read the reviewers' hostile response to Wordsworth's 1807 *Poems, in Two Volumes*, particularly the section entitled "Moods of My Own Mind," which they labeled "effeminate."

Writers of the period just preceding and following the French Revolution agree upon the insight that society will not tolerate the wish for solitude (privacy), if solitude means genuine independence. Caleb Williams, in Godwin's novel of 1794, simply cannot escape his aristocratic master, Falkland, or any of the satellite figures who together make up a cluster of eerie pursuit. Similarly the husband's pursuit of his wronged wife, Maria, in Wollstonecraft's *Maria* (1798), knows no limits. The message of each of these books is that the safe place, usually fantasized as idyllic, exists only in the mind, that the condition of modern life is to be pursued by forces of oppression, the more so if one, like Rousseau, makes his gestures of independence public knowledge. Later on Mary Shelley in *Frankenstein* and P. B. Shelley in *The Triumph of Life* quote the period's touchstone passage, from Coleridge's *The Rime of the Ancient Mariner*:

> Like one, that on a lonesome road
> Doth walk in fear and dread,
> And having once turned round walks on,
> And turns no more his head;
> Because he knows, a frightful fiend
> Doth close behind him tread.

Therefore to write a poetry of reveries, of moods of one's own mind, would flagrantly oppose the entire world of pursuit and of power.

This would be a resistance, the resistance of the feminine that is Rousseau's *Reveries*.

15

Rousseau: Calm, Solitude,
and Power

It is only after having detached myself from social passions and their sad retinue that I have again found nature with all its charm.

Convinced of the impossibility of containing these first involuntary motions, I gave up all my efforts to do so. Now, at each blow I let my blood boil. I let anger and indignation take possession of my senses. I yield this first explosion, that all my strength could neither stop nor delay, to nature. I try only to stop its consequences before it produces any effect. Flashing eyes, an inflamed face, trembling limbs, a throbbing heart—that is all purely physical, and reasoning can do nothing about it. But after having let our natural temperament have its first explosion, we can become our own master again as we regain our senses bit by bit. . . . I wait for the moment when I can conquer by letting my reason act; for it speaks to me only when it can make itself heard. Alas! What am I saying, my reason! I would be very wrong to honor it with this triumph, for it hardly plays a role in any of this. Everything comes out the same when a changeable temperament is irritated by an impetuous wind, but becomes calm again the instant the wind stops blowing. My ardent natural temperament irritates me; my indolent natural temperament pacifies me. I yield to all present impulses; every conflict sets off an intense and short motion in me. As soon as the conflict subsides, the motion ceases. Nothing imparted from outside can prolong itself in me.[1]

Rousseau claims that the symptoms of passion reside in his body's irritability around the "social passions." How different is he from his own St. Preux or Julie? At first the warring or opposing elements seem to be passion and reason. But Rousseau suddenly discovers that not reason but simply a different nature, a calming nature, asserts itself over the irritable, destabilizing one in time. Both passion and its withdrawal belong to involuntary, unwilled aspects of being. What can be willed is the orchestration of these elements so that they exert their natural antipathies in a manner which does not permanently injure or depress the self.

To bring this back to the imagery of Rousseau, if a large rock were thrown into a normally peaceful lake, it would cause an enormous turbulence and disruption of the surface (*amour propre*); but soon the definitive calm of the lake would reassert itself with its gentle, rhythmic rocking movement (*amour de soi*).

Unessential to the self, the social passions are an irritant, an unfortunate epiphenomenon of being a social person. This has dire consequences, however, for Rousseau's definition of reason. Reason works like a benign dictator, allowing the poor benighted social passions to play themselves out harmlessly in order to vanish in exhaustion: this is "wise passiveness." But reason does not stir up the social passions through its commitment to understanding and acting upon the complex human conditions that created them. In the *Reveries* (from which the above passage was taken) and *Confessions* reason becomes that faculty that delights (in solitude) in his discovery and classification of plants, the fantasy of ordering and administering, like a colonial ruler, the species of the natural world. A fantasy of domination accompanies the solitary pleasure of reason, of *amour de soi*.

16

"Emmeline" and Resistance in
Wordsworth's Lyrics

"Wordsworth's poetry, when he is at his best, is as inevitable as Nature herself."[1] In today's intellectual climate, one views Arnold's praise as an instance of what is precisely wrong with Wordsworth's lyrics: a smugness or complacency about social issues, and a psychological complexity that casts itself as natural inevitability. We can assume that Arnold, whose 1879 anthology of Wordsworth revealed an essentially lyric poet, found this inevitability primarily at the lyric dimension. But the reviewers of the 1807 *Poems, in Two Volumes*, mostly a volume of Wordsworth's now most famous and characteristic work in the lyric vein, reacted to such poetry with irritation: it was "trivial" and "effeminate," not at all inevitable. They hated a poetry of "moods," moods, moreover, of "[one's] own mind."

This fact of the reviewers makes me hesitate to join them or my contemporaries sympathetic to them in condemning or consigning to oblivion those lyrics of the *chastely beautiful*, such as "To a Butterfly" (both versions) or "The Sparrow's Nest," and by extension the poems to the daisy and the green linnet, poems with which Arnold begins his section in the anthology designated "lyrical poems." The hero, or heroine, of this section is Dorothy, or "Emmeline," a playmate who also teaches the poet how to resist his impulsiveness and his aggression:

> My Sister Emmeline and I
> Together chased the Butterfly!
> A very hunter did I rush
> Upon the prey:—with leaps and springs
> I followed on from brake to bush;
> But she, God love her! feared to brush
> The dust from off its wings.

In the second butterfly poem, he has learned his lesson:

> I've watched you now a full half-hour,
> Self-poised upon that yellow flower. . . .

Presumably this is a quality Arnold likes in one of his favorite lyrics, "The Solitary Reaper": "I listened, motionless and still. . . ."

Perhaps the reviewers called trivial and effeminate that which expressed not a wise but a resisting and *feminine* passiveness, as opposed to a "masculine" poetic aggression.

17

The Scene—I

Werther is the great novelistic display of Romantic subjectivity: the land-scape emanates as expression from the inner world of the protagonist. At times it is hard to tell where Werther ends and the landscape begins. Goethe's sympathy for his character lies in knowing that many of Werther's paranoiac observations on people and their social and economic penchants are true. (The same can be said of Rousseau in part II of the *Confessions*.)[1] While becoming the instrument for scoring the defects of capitalist society, subjectivity sacrifices the person to the coldness of that society by making him—like the single side of a Möbius strip—indistinguishable from it.

Werther's subjectivity similarly draws into itself the love of the two other main characters, Lotte and her fiancé and later husband, Albert. The deep feeling of transcendent connection from time to time spreading among them appears critical of bourgeois values but in fact confirms them by aban-doning a vision of their transformation. It is striking how much rage and hatred—culminating in Werther's helpless, violent, messy suicide—lies beneath the love. The rage marks the limits of subjectivity as insight and social connection and indicates how this subjectivity is a form of attempted appropriation and control.

Yet the final page of the novel shows that Goethe has released himself from this protagonist's subjective appropriation of the world. The "editor," himself previously caught up in Werther, suddenly, as he describes the sui-cide and its aftermath among the local society, becomes more "objective." Detail follows detail like the relentless ticking of a clock—that is, as if each detail were beyond the editor's editing power. The Romantic self van-ishes amidst the details which nonetheless are not anarchic but brought together under some new principle of organization. Characters from the novel materialize, as at the end of a traditional play, for the final *scene*.

Like the description of Rousseau ravaged by the shock of encounter with the Great Dane, the description of the dying Werther includes the Homeric (Iliadic) brutalizing of serene human form and coherence with the precise detailing of the body invaded and mutilated by the gloomy and perverse weapon of self-destruction, the gun. This loving patience of description leads directly to the final—scenic—paragraph:

> The old judge came bursting in as soon as he heard the news. With the hot tears streaming down his cheeks, he kissed the dying man. His oldest sons soon followed him on foot. They fell on their knees beside the bed in attitudes of the wildest grief, kissing the dying man's hand, his mouth. The oldest one, whom Werther had always loved best, clung to his lips as he expired and had to be forcefully removed. At twelve noon, Werther died. The presence of the judge and the arrangements he made silenced the crowd. That night, at about eleven, he had the body buried in the spot Werther had chosen. The old man and his sons walked behind the bier; Albert found himself incapable of doing so. They feared for Lotte's life. Workmen carried the body. There was no priest in attendance.[2]

This actually is the least objective or "disinterested" moment in the novel: it turns the truly anarchic and self-explosive and meaningless death of the preceding paragraphs into a socially very meaningful and coherent scene of a potentially more fruitful explosion. Werther stimulates in others a violence of emotion that by its nature and intensity defies the constraints of the dominating, bourgeois social structure. Albert, the representative of stable bourgeois order, is numb; the church that sacralizes that order is absent. The elements of social and sexual revolution are gathered in this final scene—gathered but barely *held in check*. By killing himself Werther removes the possibility of final resolution since that vision dies with him. Goethe opens up the possibility of going beyond subjectivity or through it to a "new birth," in Shelley's phrase, of fairer social organization. Part of the revolutionary tension in this scene comes from the release, at Werther's death, of enormous homoerotic passions.

[18]

The Scene—II

"It was, in truth, a scene of fairy-land."[1] Romanticism posits this other, anti-Brechtian, scene, the comic-romance ending of Ann Radcliffe's *The Italian*. If *Werther* ends with a scene of social and political tensions, *The Italian* reduces the dissonant sounds and centrifugal motions within its society to a single, final melodic line of idyllic triumph. The bourgeois imagination (secure in the lap of the transformative imagination of *The Tempest* and *The Winter's Tale*) reconciles the roving, mobile woman (Ellena) to marriage, allows the underclass servant (Paulo) pleasure in his master's superior position (remember, this is 1797), and converts the brutal, intrusive Inquisition into an instrument of justice. We are asked to believe that truth and fairyland are the same, that conflicting social and sexual elements blend together in a common humanity.

Radcliffe shows her contemporaries' awareness of the insistent powers of the preconscious (if not the unconscious) mind: intuition, association, guilty associations and predictions. One keeps expecting these to destabilize the plot, but they don't. Their access to other avenues of social life and psychological experience turns out to be sham, since the author always reveals the (comic) truths. This is "Enlightenment thinking"[2] as control, as confirmation and celebration of the existing order.

The scene in Radcliffe suggests that the imagination can resolve or *dis*solve social conflict. Or . . . should I read this more subversively? Perhaps Radcliffe, with her transparently idyllic resolutions, wants to expose the incapacity of the Romantic imagination to embrace, to order, to disarm the drives and passions of individuals in love and individuals struggling in class and gender wars. The idyllic, romance ending is so frail. The mechanisms of "conversion" of evil into good are so melodramatic. The latent class wars are so conveniently and completely resolved. Social mysteries and emotional darkness are so imperiously eradicated.

The problem with Gothic novels, said Mary Wollstonecraft, is that they "amuse while they affright."[3] Perhaps she aims her critique at Radcliffe's target: the creaky mechanisms of plot resolution. But I sense here a puritanical element in Wollstonecraft's radicalism that abuts against the release of erotically charged fantasy in Gothic plot. In the opening pages of *Maria; Or the Wrongs of Woman* she contrasts the "made-up" screams of characters in a Gothic novel, the "spectres and chimeras, conjured up by the magic spell of genius to harrow the soul, and absorb the wondering mind," with the experience of Maria, hounded by a viciously sexist husband supported by a brutally sexist society. "Fairy-land" is less potent in fiction than the extreme mental torture and physical imprisonment suffered by a woman simply seeking a degree of fulfillment and independent choice. The idyllic world—in *Maria*—constructed by the imagination is more a problem than an occasion for celebration and solution. For Wollstonecraft beauty is "une promesse de bonheur."[4] Imagination, the faculty that creates the beautiful and defines it as harmony, is activated by the prison/madhouse that Maria finds herself in. The products of her imagination—a happy marriage, a blissful romance, etc.—obviously depend upon the "bad present," but Wollstonecraft does not celebrate them. They are, however, still a promise of happiness, not necessarily the exact happiness offered (e.g., the happy marriage) but some happiness and some new possibility of pleasure and improvement.

One such possibility that Wollstonecraft envisioned in her notes for the end of this unfinished novel is the strengthening of the mother-daughter relationship, a passionate engagement with the daughter's future.

Thus the future, unlike that of the Gothic, contains a scene of conflict (the patriarchy challenged) and of hope in that conflict.

The Final Scene in Werther:

Further Thoughts

*There are some exceptions. There have always been those uncertain, poetic per-
sons who have not let themselves be reduced to dummies programmed by pitiless
repression of the homosexual element. Men or women: beings who are complex,
mobile, open. Accepting the other sex as a component makes them much richer,
more various, stronger, and—to the extent that they are mobile—very fragile.
It is only in this condition that we invent.*

—Hélène Cixous

When he hears from the peasant boy the story of his passion for the older
widow, Werther "catches fire," identifying not only with the heterosexual
passion but also, by his excitement for the boy, with the teller of the tale
of passion. When he receives from a male servant a message from Lotte and
realizes that the servant has recently been in her presence, Werther wants
to embrace him passionately. Should we then be surprised to discover that
in the final, death scene of the novel, a boy is passionately kissing the lips
of the dead Werther at the same time that "they feared for Lotte's life"?

Werther is fragile. People in the novel and surely in the history of criticism (perhaps, ambivalently, Goethe himself) deem him pathological. But
his fragility is also a mobility, and he mobilizes others. He destabilizes
this society through his transparent, partly involuntary risk of his bisexual
inclinations. Most definitely, his sexuality belongs to his social critique.
On the last page of the novel, erotic destabilization nearly tears apart the
hierarchical stability brought into focus by the rituals of death.

What would have happened had Werther refused to die?

[20]

An Idyll of Liberty

And then I felt thee!—on that sea-cliff's verge,
　　Whose pines, scarce travelled by the breeze above,
Had made one murmur with the distant surge!
Yes, while I stood and gazed, my temples bare,
And shot my being through earth, sea, and air,
　　Possessing all things with intensest love,
　　　O Liberty! my spirit felt thee there.

One anonymous reviewer from the *Critical Review* in July 1798 remarked, about the above concluding passage from Coleridge's "France: An Ode": "What does Mr. Coleridge mean by liberty in this passage? or what connexion has it with the subject of civic freedom?" [1] The author is saying that the word has gone through a transformation in the poem, that in a poem beginning with the French Revolution it would bear its common, predictable, and historically charged social meaning but that it has by the end slipped into the asocial context of the natural world. The Romantics, of course, celebrate this discovery of liberty-in-solitude, but the reviewer asks whether the word has not, in its new setting, lost its meaning altogether. Indeed, he might have gone on to ask the same question about the use of "love" in this passage, love in this case not even demanding the presence of another human being. According to the conventional Romantic wisdom—begun by Coleridge in the prose summary of "France: An Ode" and confirmed for us, nearly a hundred fifty years later, in M. H. Abrams' classic essays—the transformation of the individual out of his political or public role and toward love and solitude is itself a radical political act: it can loosen the organizing principle of modern society—power—which it replaces with love. However, Coleridge's domestic poems written mostly from 1795 to 1798 enact what John Sitter (writing about the eighteenth-century lyric) has called a "flight from history" and therefore pitch the individual permanently away from history toward the preferred idyll of the imagination in retirement. Here beauty can be recovered by the poet, under the protective encouragement of Nature:

> Henceforth I shall know
> That Nature ne'er deserts the wise and pure;
> No plot so narrow, be but Nature there,
> No waste so vacant, but may well employ
> Each faculty of sense, and keep the heart
> Awake to Love and Beauty!
> ("This Lime-Tree Bower My Prison")

Is it necessary that beauty emerge only with the poet's flight from history?
That would be a chaste beauty indeed.

21

"Colouring of Imagination"

Wordsworth chose, he said, to write in the language of the "low and rustic" since they lived more closely to the "essential passions" and according to the "primary laws of our nature"; "in that condition of life our elementary feelings co-exist in a state of greater simplicity. . . ." Poetry, further, should give pleasure to a reader not defined in a social role "as a Man." This is essentialism.

Yet the essential, we are told, is not the same as the "ordinary" or the familiar since the poet has sought "to throw over [incidents and situations from common life] a certain colouring of imagination, whereby ordinary things should be presented to the mind in an unusual way. . . ." Similarly, to "get down to essentials" is to exclude the nonessential. It is a paring away, a reduction from many to the one. But apparently one reduces to one by adding something: the coloring of imagination.

Wordsworth uses the word "to throw" as in throwing a coat or a shawl over one's shoulder, placing a barrier or distance between the "naked and native" self, the specificity of self, and the social world. Blake despised the colorists because they deemphasized the outlines that supposedly capture the self in his or her social particularity. Color seduces the eye away from difference to sameness, our "humanity." From a distance we are all the same. From the "pleasing prospect" of essentialist poetry, we can appropriate the poetic object for ourselves, possess it and feel sublimely safe, sublimely rich, sublimely sad that the agonies of ordinary people (e.g., those in *Lyrical Ballads* or *The Ruined Cottage*) can appear so beautiful and permanent.

I feel the sentiment of existence when the ordinary lives of others, when politics and history, are cloaked in color, far away.

But I have been forced to discover that the association of poetic beauty with this coloring of imagination thrown over objects exists in a less pure political context. In an exchange between Edmund Burke and Mary Wollstonecraft the image of the cloak becomes the occasion for fierce debate between the values of continuity in present "civilization" and those of the "rights of man." For Burke the capture and execution of King Louis XVI symbolize the brutality of the Revolutionaries against nothing less than civilization, an abhorrent change depicted in the imagery of drapery:

> But now all is to be changed. All the pleasing illusions, which made power gentle, and obedience liberal, which harmonized the different shades of life, and which, by a bland assimilation, incorporated into politics the sentiments which beautify and soften private society, are to be dissolved by this new conquering empire of light and reason. All the decent drapery of life is to be rudely torn off. All the super-added ideas, furnished from the wardrobe of a moral imagination, which the heart owns, and the understanding ratifies, as necessary to cover the defects of our naked shivering nature, and to raise it to dignity in our own estimation, are to be exploded as a ridiculous, absurd, and antiquated fashion.[1]

Several pages earlier Burke has fashioned the fall of the king and the queen, the entry into their chambers and their capture, as a rape of royalty—a violation of dignity, nobility, beauty, and civilization reminiscent of the fall of Troy in the *Aeneid*. Burke insists that not only is the attack on royalty unnatural, but it is also perverse, immoral—a rape. Burke, in other words, makes the association of revolutionary action and sexual passion that the radicals (like Blake) do, but sees in it desecration and not liberation. And here the Virgilian association shades into a Freudian one: the "drapery of life" is the necessary illusion, the necessary defense against the rawness of nature; even if life consists of discontinuities, of abrupt and frightening changes, the drapery of manners and custom insures a consoling beauty in continuity.

Mary Wollstonecraft in *A Vindication of the Rights of Man* challenges not so much the need for illusions as the particular use that Burke and other "gentlemen" make of it:

> But it was the poor man with only his native dignity who was thus oppressed—and only metaphysical sophists and cold mathematicians can discern this insubstantial form; it is a work of abstraction—and a *gentleman* of lively imagination must borrow some drapery from fancy before he can love or pity a *man*.—Misery, to reach your heart, I perceive, [she says to Burke] must have its cap and bells; your tears are reserved, very *naturally* considering your character, for the declamation of the theatre, or for the downfall of queens, whose rank alters

the nature of folly, and throws a graceful veil over vices that degrade humanity; whilst the distress of many industrious mothers, whose *helpmates* have been torn from them, and the hungry cry of helpless babes, were vulgar sorrows that could not move your commiseration, though they might extort an alms.[2]

What Burke contended was the beneficent illusion of civilization is for Wollstonecraft the chosen illusion of the wealthy and the nobility, allowing them to avoid the facts of poverty. She shatters the essentialist fantasy, that we are all "human."

Which brings us back to Wordsworth and his coloring of imagination thrown over the objects of his concern, the rural poor and dispossessed. Like the radical artist Blake, Wordsworth here believes in the supremacy of form, or outline, over color (even if it is coloring of imagination). But he would have that color usurp the place of form in importance. Does this mean that beauty in poetry must deny the distinctions in, for example, class? Does it mean, to pursue the drapery image, that beauty exists solely in the service of principles of continuity and status quo? and that that which is beautiful, like the queen of France, is female, an object of men's fantasies? Or, to take Wordsworth at his word, does the coloring of imagination *defamiliarize* the object in order to call its particular fate to the attention of a society sated with excess stimulation?

22

Thelwall, Coleridge, and

Domestic Poetry

John Thelwall, hounded for several years by British government agents and angry citizens, finally sought relief in the summer of 1797 in the idyllic rural society of Coleridge at Nether Stowey. Several of Thelwall's poems written at this time record the longing of the exhausted and persecuted radical for some private peace, for some companionship that would nurture the exuberance of his mind, and for an art form that could save him from his history and the contentiousness of society. Coleridge must have known these poems by the time he wrote "This Lime-Tree Bower My Prison" and certainly by the time of "Frost at Midnight" and "The Nightingale." Very likely he conceived these poems as answers to Thelwall (although "Reflections on Having Left a Place of Retirement," similar to the later domestic poems, was written in 1795).

The similarities between Thelwall's relatively unknown poems and Coleridge's domestic poems are immediately apparent. Thelwall writes in solitude or addresses one or more sympathetic companions. He focuses on the pleasures of the idyllic life to which he contrasts the life of society at large, taking that life both in the abstract and, autobiographically, in his own experience. "On Leaving the Bottoms of Gloucestershire; where the Author had been entertained by several families with Great Hospitality. Aug. 12, 1797"[1] is about separation, like "This Lime-Tree Bower," and like "The Nightingale" is about the resistance to separation from friends:

> Once again,
> Then, once again, and my full heart no more
> Lingering shall falter—once again, farewell—
> Dear scenes of hospitality and joy!—
> A long farewell. . . .[2]

"To the Infant Hampden" of October 1797, the monologue about rural peace and past social agony and disruption, has as its primary reference Thelwall's sleeping infant, just as does "Frost at Midnight" (January 1798), and places a wish in the future life of his son free of the disabling complexities brought on by an evil world:

> Ah! sleep secure:
> And may thy dream of Life be ne'er disturb'd
> With visions such as mar thy father's peace——[3]

And in "Maria" (October 1797) the language recalling his imprisonment for treason in 1794 anticipates the schoolboy passage of "Frost at Midnight":

> When thro' my grated dungeon I have gaz'd,
> With straining eye unmov'd, upon the gate
> Thro' which the partner of my soul should pass——
> And this, my only babe. . . .[4]

These poems were written when Thelwall was in the country, on a trip to find a rural retreat for his family, a trip taken alone. This voluntary though enforced separation is referred to poignantly in the poems. The passage above about his prison term resonates to the present separation from his family. This in turn creates the more general atmosphere of his status in society: a lonely and homeless wanderer, a man of good intentions who is cut down, persecuted, disavowed. The poems touch one of the themes of radical literature in the 1790s and early 1800s from *Caleb Williams* and *The Borderers* to *Frankenstein*:

> Yet must I leave
> Your social haunts—for not my unblest feet
> Yet may I rest, or my long wanderings close,
> Tho weary'd: but thro' many an untried scene
> (Perhaps from this how differing!) shape my way,
> Beneath my weight of sorrows. . . .[5]

> the tired foot
> Of persecuted Virtue cannot find
> One spray on which to rest; or scarce one leaf
> To cheer with promise of subsiding woe.[6]

Coleridge had experienced persecution to a lesser degree and sympathized with Thelwall's experience and burden. He felt the threat of more persecution with the presence of Thelwall in the neighborhood. Yet his poems reflect none of this social reality. Even in "Fears in Solitude" (early 1798), the one poem in which he declares government's criticism of his political statements and inclinations, he refers that criticism ultimately back to the security of his domestic life. He weaves in Thelwallian themes only to deny reference to their original political and personal significance. Thelwall's poem of separation from friends refers to a probably permanent separation based on the fact of his wandering, persecuted state, but Coleridge's "The Nightingale" turns separation into the most casual and routine of daily occurrences, one that will be reversed by seeing Dorothy and William Wordsworth the next morning. In "This Lime-Tree Bower" Coleridge annuls the separation from his friend Charles Lamb through the imagination's elaboration on the rook flying in common view.

Separation, in other words, represents the political condition of the radical in the 1790s. It also represents the condition of one dispossessed of land or domestic security. It is not enough to say that such figures are wanderers or simply alienated beings. They are often persecuted as well. This means not only that they are lonely or misunderstood, but that their loneliness has the claustral burdens of the political prisoner. From this point of view Coleridge's use of imagination (while having its own tradition in the nature poetry of solitude in the eighteenth century) becomes a solution to the plight of the persecuted radical. For not only is loneliness annulled by imagination, but it is turned into a virtue. In the midst of separation the imagination flourishes and can exercise its nourishing power. Thus when Coleridge, separated in the lime-tree bower from his friends, can moralize:

> Henceforth I shall know
> That Nature ne'er deserts the wise and pure;
> No plot so narrow, be but Nature there,
> No waste so vacant, but may well employ
> Each faculty of sense, and keep the heart
> Awake to Love and Beauty!

he is transforming separation from a condition of political persecution to a newly preferred condition of being—the solitary "liberty" of contemplation and the feeling of love.

Thelwall's actual imprisonment or enforced separation becomes rationalized metaphorically into "the happy prison." At times, for example in Wollstonecraft's *Maria*—written the same year as "This Lime-Tree Bower"—the "freedom" achieved by the imagination of the prisoner is recognized as an illusion. Just as Thelwall views domestic retirement as a longing and not a reality, so the prisoner Maria does not see the imagination as an actual liberation. But not only does Coleridge enact the imagination freeing itself totally from its prison, but the prison, a lime-tree bower, obviously isn't one. The imagination, in this sense, achieves its victory over a specious opposition by substituting for contemporary radical politics the preference for nature, spirit, and communion. Similarly, in "Frost at Midnight" Coleridge transforms Thelwall's painful lines about vainly looking out of his prison bars for his family into lines about a child in school who, "Awed by the stern preceptor's face," "snatched / A hasty glance" and "hoped to see the *stranger's* face, / Townsman, or aunt, or sister more beloved, / My playmate when we both were clothed alike!" The school becomes a prison for his imagination, barring him from the pleasure of companionship.

In addition, *the revolutionary adolescent or young adult* (in Thelwall) *has been replaced in Coleridge's poem by a much younger child.* A socially committed and passionate being has yielded to a child who barely knows sexual difference, whose longings are pure instinct unmediated by understanding and choice. A scene of the experience of political oppression in Thelwall becomes in Coleridge a scene that delivers a common early Romantic message: modern education imprisons and destroys the pure spiritual exuberance of childhood.

23

Thelwall, Coleridge, and

Nature's Rescue

Anxiously questioning in his poems his future (will he be hounded by government and suspicious persons or protected in rural ease?), Thelwall portrays a mind exposed and vulnerable. The play of mind in Coleridge, like the play of a child, assumes a protection from consequence. In a poem like "Frost at Midnight" the representation of nature ritualistically creates the protection. The descriptions of nature, among the memorable and defining elements of the domestic poems and exercising most originally the poet's talent, are totally absent in Thelwall. Longing for the idyll of nature, Thelwall cannot seem to possess it in words: most of Thelwall's poems, and particularly the nature passages, are written merely in stock eighteenth-century diction. Apparently the best poetic language of the time demanded a total commitment to what was for some Romantics a preferred condition of being, not only the hunger for it—thus the evocative and authenticating opening lines of "Frost at Midnight": "The Frost performs its secret ministry, / Unhelped by any wind."

In his poem to his sleeping child, Thelwall states his separation from wife and child and the persecution which has created it. His cries acknowledge his estrangement by government agencies of repression and by societal superstitions. Coleridge's opening lines to his child displace these agencies onto nature. The natural agency is secret, solitary, a mysterious prime mover. The phrase "secret ministry" confuses religious and political associations. It alludes to a healing power, coming from the outside and bestowed upon the speaking voice. "Performs" suggests a performance, a staging of an event, an artwork, not—however—by the human subject, who is at once patient and spectator, or observer. Parenthetically, Coleridge in 1797 wrote of Thelwall, whom he liked "uncommonly well": "*Energetic Activity,* of mind and of *heart,* is his Master-feature. He is prompt to *conceive,* and still prompter to *execute*—. But I think, that he is deficient in that *patience* of mind, which can look *intensely* and *frequently* at the same subject." [1] To push these connections further, Coleridge resists the radical's mind—active, restless, and always seeking to be effectual—and prefers the patient mind, the mind that suspends its *belief*. Does not he in this stance make himself the patient, before a healing power?

This same animistic use of language ("frost," not the human subject, does the performing), what Max Horkheimer calls the "hypostatization of states and actions as nominatives," perhaps finds its most memorable and convincing Romantic instance six years later in the great consoling passages of Wordsworth's "Immortality Ode" where "*Nature* yet remembers" and "*faith* looks through death."

Thelwall, by contrast, does no more than imagine, yearn for, imagination and measure the choices reality presents to him. Thelwall's endeavor looks meager indeed, supporting Donald Reiman's assessment of Thelwall's poetic language (applying Hazlitt's phrase for Thelwall's prose), that it is a "mere drab-coloured suit."²

Everything, in Coleridge's domestic poems, seems to point to a requirement that poetic beauty emerge in a "flight from history." Does beauty also appear only with a flight from passion and desire? I am tempted to agree to both formulae; that would allow for a neat critical symmetry or proportion: Romantic beauty is inversely proportional to historical and social commitment and to the representation of eros. Furthermore, it would fit with the judgment about Thelwall's language: the committed writer throws only a drab coloring over the incidents his words describe. But passages in Coleridge's poems are so rich and alive, so full of motion, so full of sympathetic identification that to feel that their beauty has not subsumed passion seems a serious denial of the experience of reading them.

"This Lime-Tree Bower" and "The Nightingale," for example, contain passages of natural description that seem less like a poetry of escape or "retirement" and more a poetry of ecstatic and absorbed presence:

> Ah! slowly sink
> Behind the western ridge, thou glorious sun!
> Shine in the slant beams of the sinking orb,
> Ye purple heath-flowers! richlier burn, ye clouds!
> Live in the yellow light, ye distant groves!
> And kindle, thou blue ocean!
>
> Pale beneath the blaze
> Hung the transparent foliage; and I watched
> Some broad and sunny leaf, and loved to see
> The shadow of the leaf and stem above

Dappling its sunshine! And that walnut-tree
Was richly tinged, and a deep radiance lay
Full on the ancient ivy, which usurps
Those fronting elms, and now, with blackest mass
Makes their dark branches gleam a lighter hue
Through the late twilight. . . .

What is the relationship here between, in John Brenkman's phrase, "lyric and society"? Coleridge has in common with Thelwall the recognition of a condition of alienation at the beginning of this poem ("Well, they are gone . . ."). But Coleridge tries to establish a lyric "utopia" by the end of the poem by asserting the connection between the two physically separated friends through their both observing the same rook crossing the path of the sun. Let me note again that Thelwall has no descriptive passages comparable to Coleridge's. How does the above description contribute to this utopian end?

The representation of nature, first of all, is not added to the representation of the human relationship but fundamental to it. At the same time nature appears in the poem because of the poet's alienation from his friends. In the act of such an analysis I am caught responding to contradictory poetic impulses, a dilemma—by the way—not experienced in the naive act of reading the poem: does Coleridge revert from his relationship with his friend to the substitute, more solipsistic engagement with natural description? or does nature "serve" the human relationship? The dilemma works within the description itself: does the sunlight cloak the branches and leaves in a Burkean/Wordsworthian manner, or does it radiate from the tree itself? In one sense the light obviously comes from the sun to the object, but the effect of the language suggests that the poet experiences the opposite. Put differently, there are opposing metaphors operating here: "Light is outer" versus "Light is inner." The poet accepts the ambiguity through his intense empathy with the situation; his passion for the illusion, for the phenomenal experience, overwhelms the "objective" fact. As in Stendhal's "crystallization" of the lover's desire for his or her beloved, the intensity of the illusion is the "truth" of the event. Perhaps this can explain why "This Lime-Tree Bower My Prison," more than any of the more overtly political and nakedly historical poems of John Thelwall, leads us toward a sense of greater human and social possibility. Through the lyric, we have been given a beauty dependent not on "retirement" but on "engagement."

24

Thelwall: Denying Politics, Creating

the Romantic Self

In a famous *Table Talk* entry of 1830 Coleridge recalls of Thelwall: "We were once sitting in a beautiful recess in the Quantocks, when I said to him, 'Citizen John, this is a fine place to talk treason in!' 'Nay, Citizen Samuel,' replied he, 'it is rather a place to make a man forget that there is any necessity for treason!' " [1] Near the end of the "Bridgewater" poem, Thelwall longs to yield to domestic life:

> its mild cares
> And stingless extasies; while gentle Sleep,
> Unwoo'd, uncall'd, on the soft pillow waits
> Of envyless Obscurity.[2]

Although he obviously joins ranks with the "flight from history" poets of the mid-eighteenth century, his particular history makes this wish for oblivion particularly poignant. Thelwall's language and thought ironically do not obliterate the history he wishes to deny or surpass. The Romantic category of forgetting is, for him, just another fantasy. Coleridge's poems are actually written in the paradoxically eroticized language of the forgotten: utterances of musings, whisperings, mutterings, breathings. They often imply that to forget the habits of mind and feeling that accrue around an immediate involvement in society brings one closer to a preferred condition of being.

When he published in 1801 the poems I have discussed as *Poems chiefly written in Retirement*, Thelwall wrote a "Prefatory Memoir" to the volume which shows his strenuous exertions to transform his reputation from that of a radical activist to that of a literary contemplative. "It is the Man, and not the Politician, that is here delineated," he began, "the disciple of the Muses; not the Lecturer and Leader of Popular Societies now no more. . . . he is desirous that the politician should be forgotten; and that, till the prejudices of party shall subside into the candour of unimpassioned appreciation, he should henceforth be known and noticed (as here he is introduced) only as a candidate for poetical and moral reputation."[3]

This same conspiracy was taken up by his second wife who, in November 1838, wrote to Wordsworth the following letter requesting information for part of a biography of her husband: "Of course I do not wish to have any political reference to the acquaintance which then subsisted between you; but merely of that communion of kindred minds, which poetry and literature linked in the bonds of Friendship."[4] Autobiographical writing, in Thelwall, Wordsworth, and Coleridge, concretizes the notion of an essential self, fundamentally not socially disruptive and not defined through its political relations. That self is confirmed, rescued into coherence by benign interventions from nature—a nature which surrounds the self in a stream, or a cloak, of what Geoffrey Hartman has recently called a "euphemia" of language. In his Prefatory Memoir Thelwall reveals with all sincerity that his association with literature is the primary identifying feature of his life, while politics intruded itself upon an unwilling subject. In turn his "diseased enthusiasm" allowed him but fitful access to his literary inclinations and produced mental exhaustion.

Yet the poems reveal that, in the midst of this politically determined journey, Thelwall—unlike the Coleridge of the domestic poems—maintained his skepticism about poetry's capacity, the capacity of beauty, to remake the quality of his experience;

> "Fortune waft you on your way!"
>   Sighs the nymph—but sighs in vain.
> Fortune turns another way:
>   Verse and Beauty plead in vain.

But who—Thelwall or Coleridge—finally had the more capacious, the more liberated idea of beauty?

25

Judgment and Disinterestedness—I

Rousseau's autobiographical writings are exhibits of loneliness. Intimacy and relationship generally get distanced by the wish for a favorable posthumous judgment on his character: a posthumous conviction that he celebrated within himself, and lived by, the sentiment of existence. I feel his loneliness in his testy, defiant, provocative attitude to his reader. Look, he says, at my outrageous and perverse insufficiencies: castigate me for the *deed* but make not the deed the basis of your final judgment but rather my soul which is pure. My perverse acts do not result from evil *intentions*. Not my acts but the innocence and goodness of my intentions, based on the goodness of my soul, should mold your judgment.

But is it not by actions that we establish our intimacies? Does not the rhetoric of intention finally prove cold? and preserve our loneliness?

"Disinterestedness" is the version in aesthetics of judgments based upon intention. The disinterested observer judges the object not on the basis of its social or psychological effects. In literary criticism this usually leads to analysis of the internal relations of the object and judgment of the degree of coherence of all its parts. If the art object can be lonely, this is what that would mean. But finally the loneliness would be cemented in the disinterested viewer, which he (or, less likely these days, she) would be surprised to discover.

26

Judgment and Disinterestedness—II:
The Walker

Wordsworth appears disinterested in "The Solitary Reaper," observing—with eye and ear—the woman sing and reap alone in the field but remaining at a substantial distance from her. He wants to know the substance of her song: is it curiosity that fixes him upon her? does he need to possess the song? does he somewhere feel implicated in it?—after all, they are both alone. The male feels the hunger for that distant female reassurance:

> Will no one tell me what she sings?—
> Perhaps the plaintive numbers flow
> For old, unhappy, far-off things,
> And battles long ago:
> Or is it some more humble lay,
> Familiar matter of to-day?
> Some natural sorrow, loss, or pain,
> That has been, and may be again?

The poet only momentarily forgets that he is a walker. Although he is initially drawn to a halt by the melancholy beauty-as-comfort of her song and body, the power assumed in his own hunger for a response, from her or another, seems to remind him to forget the questions and move on. Better she remain a picture, some music:

> And, as I mounted up the hill,—
> The music in my heart I bore,
> Long after it was heard no more.

Now he strangely appropriates the feminine comfort to himself, bearing the music, as burden but also as child. The words of the song, that which would make the woman a subject, dissolve, by his insistence on keeping them unknown, into music. The immanence of voice linked to the body yields to the transcendence of *lied: die schöne Müllerin*. The woman appears only to disappear into the disinterested "heart" of the male walker.

There is a Kafka paragraph about a city walker who sees at night on an empty street one man chasing another.[1] Like Wordsworth, Kafka asks questions about them, which amount to: is, or is not, one man in danger? And then, like Wordsworth but with a modern comic bitterness, dissolves the questions, excusing himself for having drunk too much and its being late, and walks on.

Camus's *The Fall*, according to Shoshana Felman an allegory about the difficulty of being a witness to the Holocaust, pushes into the present the Romantic image of the walker as one at once disinterested and participating in event. The narrator walking along the banks of the Seine hears a woman commit suicide by jumping (the solitary leaper) into the river. He hears and does nothing. Then he's not sure what he has heard and refuses, for several days, to read newspapers that might tell of the episode. He refuses to know what he can know. Brutally, he becomes disinterested, more taken with a distance, an absence, than with the facts of the case. None of these narrators goes the distance in bearing witness, in owning up to their evident though involuntary implicatedness in the social event.

But where does ideology (Wordsworth, the pleasure of the beautiful woman, of such solitude) end and psychology (Kafka's fear of possible reprisal against himself, Camus's narrator's denial of unspeakably horrible events) begin?

Perhaps behind Wordsworth's disinterested pleasure in the solitary reaper lies the 1792 trauma of bearing witness to the holocaust scene of the September Massacres, the Carousel itself vague and emptied of event as he looks down upon it, unable to "read" its contents. He bears witness to his inability to know the event and his relationship to it or implicatedness in it. Next to the September Massacres lay for Wordsworth the apparent emotional holocaust of separation from Annette Vallon brought on at least in part by her royalist father's rejection of her republican boyfriend. Disinterestedness may mean appropriation and control, even intrusiveness. It may also mean, in Robert Lifton's phrase, psychic numbing,[2] becoming "an imbecile mind."

Afterthought. I realize that I have been so engaged by the poet's rhetoric of elegy and comfort in distance that his own erotic arousal at the reaper's song nearly (gently) passed me by:

> A voice so thrilling ne'er was heard
> In spring-time from the Cuckoo-bird. . . .

Lyric Reflections on Youth:
A Pattern in Goethe, Coleridge,
Wordsworth, Shelley

The poem begins as a meditation on the present (locodescriptive in Coleridge, reflective on change in Wordsworth, apostrophic and imperative in Goethe and Shelley).* All the poems are about change, at some point from past to present, and eventually from present to future. Some (Coleridge and Wordsworth) see the future as more permanently stable and happy than the present, the others (Goethe and Shelley) see change resulting from contested struggle and risk. Some (Goethe and Shelley) locate themselves at the center of the change: they will insure it by assertion, vision, appropriate skill. Others (Coleridge and Wordsworth) locate someone else as the prime mover, rather as the one in whom a sentiment of existence will reside and spread backward and outward to the currently incomplete poet.

In all instances the poet interrupts the intensity of preoccupation in the present to engage his own past, a highly poetic engagement. The past isn't sheer autobiography told to the reader for its intrinsic interest. Rather it creates the tensions of metaphor and comparison thinking which here get imbued with a sense of personal crisis. My past is like my present, different but not cut off from it. (Cf. Wordsworth's apostrophe to nature: "Forbode not any severing of our loves!") Goethe's Prometheus now defies the Zeus that stifled him in his youth. The act of defiance creates the metaphor of the past life. All the other poets, whatever their politics, follow Goethe in that the evocation of the past redefines the present and future as a challenge. Can love, peace, creativity, a new society be more realized for and through me? I hereby declare in the beauty of poetry, the sacred space of poetry, my willingness to risk myself in the examined life, by turning my past life into metaphor that lives only in the present, that turns the past into a challenge. I declare my uncertainty about my life, but also my willingness to risk it for whatever matters.

*I am thinking of Goethe's "Prometheus," Coleridge's "Frost at Midnight," Wordsworth's "Tintern Abbey," and Shelley's "Ode to the West Wind."

[28]

Lucy and TV

I just tried an interesting experiment. I turn on the TV, open an anthology of poetry and read a few lines, noting action and words on screen. I throw away some duds but the hits are impressive. Just try it.

'A violet by a mossy stone half hidden from the eye.' Wordsworth/ *Lucy poems*. There's a flower on screen right now.

'How dull it is to make an end / to rust unburnished not to shine in use.' Tennyson/*Ulysses*. On screen a cowhand is explaining to the girl he doesn't want to be *tied down*. He wants to keep moving like a tumbleweed.

'And never lifted up a single stone.' Wordsworth/*Michael*. On screen some woman is rubbing on her hand cream. No stone lifting for her. . . .

It seems like our entire sensory input is pre-programmed.

. . . It is written. Snip. Snip. Cut it up.[1]

Romantic ideology is the pre-program. William Burroughs' cut-ups show neither disrespect for the famous lines nor displeasure in them. But he cuts the ideological line that has tied us to them: the line of inflated beauty, the line of inflated tragedy.

Conversion in The Prelude

In *The Prelude* the imagination ("reason in its most exalted mood") turns the world into a map of coherence and beauty. Natural strangeness or indifference, historical difference and immediacy become "types and symbols of Eternity," letters and utterances from a transcendent, modestly unsettling, but primarily comforting source. The imagination resolves all of the psychological confusion that, in progressive Romantic literature, often signals social criticism.

The "stolen boat" passage, where the child rows lustily onto a lake only to be then admonished by the appearance of an enormous mountain striding (in response to his lusty rowing) after him, is usually given "oedipal" meaning. The "act of stealth and troubled pleasure" leads to its exposure and limitation. This kind of oedipal drama is supposed to encourage the socialization of the male child, to usher him into a more ordinary (as opposed to grandiose) consciousness. If it does not make things smoother or easier for the child, it at least puts him in touch with more of the contending forces in life. Ideally, subversively, the child should grow in his awareness and acceptance of difference, of other subjects. But in Wordsworth these changes do not directly occur. Instead of turning toward the protosociety of family or friends, he is "troubled" by his dreams, in solitude and without moorings. Huge, unknown forms move around him. Nameless, they remain permanently inchoate, a presence that cannot become a power to him. Or, as Coleridge might say, a power that cannot become a strength. The oedipal chastening takes him into sublime mystery, the troubled comfort of solitude.

But what of the wrenching passions ordinarily produced in the oedipal conflict? Unavailable, in *The Prelude*, for full expression in either erotic love or social criticism (where they usually appear in Romanticism), they sink into that shadowy but sinister word that dots book I of Wordsworth's poem: "trouble." Meanwhile the imagination, Wordsworth claims, converts experience into art, the contradictory into the idyll, thought into spirit. The father's counterforce to the child's lust for conquest and knowledge and his wish for omnipotence supports only the substitute reality of words, leaving the social and passional center of the child's world hollow, shadowy.

The poet Wordsworth later, seeming to lack an internalized image of a real father, tries to act—in poetry—like his ego ideal of a father: one who awesomely but benignly converts the troublesome powers of intimacy, nature, and society into harmonious utterance.

When the Poet experienced the loss of his favorite brother, John, he described the effect of successfully completing his grief work in an image of the self that reflected the rigidities behind the harmonies of the conversion: Peele Castle, a "rugged Pile" battered by waves, "cased in the unfeeling armour of old time." No longer is there a place for the Other. The poet, therefore, has no longer the great range of feelings (beyond idyllic "love") for the Other.

The Gothic church, Wordsworth's metaphor for his grand philosophical poem, was described by Goethe as paradoxically in its enormous size and bulk giving the appearance of airiness, of its potential for transcending the worldly. But becoming conscious of the limits to experience under the "Romantic ideology," I can once again feel the heaviness of the church's cold stones.

[30]
"*Society*"

And after lonely sojourning
In such a quiet and surrounded nook,
This burst of prospect, here the shadowy main,
Dim-tinted, there the mighty majesty
Of that huge amphitheatre of rich
And elmy fields, seems like society—
Conversing with the mind, and giving it
A livelier impulse and a dance of thought!
        (Coleridge, "Fears in Solitude")

Hence life, and change, and beauty, solitude
More active, even, than 'best society,'
Society made sweet as solitude
By silent inobtrusive sympathies,
And gentle agitations of the mind
From manifold distinctions, difference
Perceived in things, where to the common eye,
No difference is; and hence, from the same source
Sublimer joy. . . .
        (Wordsworth, *1805 Prelude*, II, 313–21)

The mind of man is fram'd even like the breath
And harmony of music. There is a dark
Invisible workmanship that reconciles
Discordant elements, and makes them move
In one society.
        (Wordsworth, *1805 Prelude*, I, 351–55)

Milton's Adam (*Paradise Lost*, IX, 227 ff.), trying to persuade Eve to make delight in each other's company as central as labor, says—nearly casually:

> But if much converse perhaps
> Thee satiate, to short absence I could yield.
> For solitude sometimes is best society,
> And short retirement urges sweet return.

Coleridge's and Wordsworth's metaphor is not casual at all but represents an effort to convert the social and civic into an amphitheater of mind, where differences are aesthetic in their significance, producing the pleasure of the sense of self-realization or completion. The mind moves in gentle agitations, like Rousseau's boat rocking gently on his Swiss lake. Thought doesn't engage in fight (Blake) but dances: "And then my heart with pleasure fills, / And dances with the daffodils."

31

"An Act of Stealth and
Troubled Pleasure": "Society"
Once More

Why does the stolen boat passage appeal so much to readers of Wordsworth?—presumably because, like all great poems of psychological precision, this one reminds us just how present the dramas of childhood are for us as grown-ups. This one also leaves us with a tension between the experience described, the opening up of the shelter of childhood, and the resolution or completion of the experience, its translation into the further life of the child that eventually (all too quickly!) becomes the life of the grown-up reading the poem. How does the act of stealth and troubled pleasure get translated to us? Wordsworth, of course, is describing an archetype—the curious, energetic innocent compelled and compelling him- or herself toward the secret and the unknown, and reaching outward by stealing something. It is also the archetype of transgression, of the testing of authority, which later on in adolescence becomes imbued with a sense of competing authorities including the nascent one within the adolescent self. Indeed, the troubled pleasure might be said to belong, archetypally, to any moment when one feels driven in the midst of competing authorities. The trouble comes from the sense of consequence, the pleasure from the sense of answering fully to one's inner drives. It is a point when, to revert to the Romantic context, "pleasure," usually associated with an idyllic resolution or submission, seems to invade the territory of destabilizing experience. It is a point when "trouble" might translate outward to simply the condition of a life conscious of the competing claims in society.

But the pattern of the poet's life built into *The Prelude* demands that "troubled pleasure" give way to a passage referred to above, to a harmony of different terms:

> The mind of man is fram'd even like the breath
> And harmony of music. There is a dark
> Invisible workmanship that reconciles
> Discordant elements, and makes them move

In one society. Ah me! that all
The terrors, all the early miseries
Regrets, vexations, lassitudes, that all
The thoughts and feelings which have been infus'd
Into my mind, should ever have made up
The calm existence that is mine when I
Am worthy of myself ! Praise to the end!

(1805, I, 351–61)

The myriad of troubled pleasures and the specific events that engendered them exist to submit to, be consumed by, a higher order of being. The invisible ("inscrutable" in 1850) workman converts discord to concord, troubled pleasure, presumably, to peace.

Brilliantly, Wordsworth exploits one of the most highly charged "key words" of his epoch: "society." Society was of course seen as the enemy to the Romantic self, the source of discord in a person's life, impersonal and dull in its power. Here it becomes, through the trick of metaphor, the ally of the self. The self is no longer active and passionate and engaged, but "calm," "made up" or composed (created but also made calm) by that invisible or inscrutable figure. Do I push the metaphor too far if I conclude:

1. if society and this new self reinforce each other, then political, critical consciousness dissolves;

2. if troubled pleasures and vexations or passions yield to calm existence, then the energy for critical consciousness also dissolves?

And yet what right do I have to dispute Wordsworth's (and before him Rousseau's) conviction in the energy, the "grand elementary principle of pleasure," provided by that sense of power in the beauty of a harmony of being? Since "pleasure" is an "elementary principle," a "troubled pleasure" (pleasure modified) would be a disturbance, an intrusion, not essential to pleasure itself.

32

A *Moment of Recalcitrance*
in The Prelude

The problem of the monogamous ideal, says Karen Horney, is twofold: From the point of view of the id the wish to obtain sexually the parent of the opposite sex can never be fulfilled in the marriage partner since that partner is recognized as a substitute for the real thing. From the point of view of the superego, seeing the marriage partner as the desired parent stimulates the incest taboo that prohibits the attainment of real pleasure.[1] We might apply this problem to *The Prelude* since "marriage" is one of Wordsworth's primary metaphors for ideal human experience.

Consider book VI of *The Prelude*, not solely for the famous Simplon Pass passage but also for what I see as the exactly parallel Lake Como passage. Taken together they create and expose a problem of the limits of a life marked by the conquest of the world by imagination; they can be seen as the wish to discover marriage as the type of complete human experience and as a disappointment of that experience.

In both cases nature presents itself as a mystery, bewilderment forced upon the adventurous traveler. "Nature," in book VI, may be a displacement from society in revolutionary France, the geographical and historical setting for these two passages. In the Simplon Pass section Wordsworth determines that Imagination—an idealizing faculty—has at once led him to misread or deny the signs in nature that would have prevented its mystery and also in the eventuality saved him from seeing nature as mysterious or indifferent by converting it into a kind of symphony or poem of mind:

> all like workings of one mind, the features
> Of the same face, blossoms upon one tree,
> Characters of the great Apocalypse,
> The types and symbols of Eternity,
> Of first, and last, and midst, and without end.
> (VI, 568–72)

Imagination conquers, possesses nature through this dramatic, visionary conversion. It makes nature *known*.

Yet this victory of imagination, which one thinks would have satisfied the poet's yearnings for the possessive, permanent, secure side of the marriage with nature, has not satisfied him. Less than a hundred lines later, he describes the visit to Lake Como where again nature mystifies him (makes him think it is near morning when in fact it is the middle of the night): we

> Were lost, bewilder'd among woods immense,
> Where, having wander'd for a while, we stopp'd
> And on a rock sate down, to wait for day.
> An open place it was, and overlook'd
> From high, the sullen water underneath,
> On which a dull red image of the moon
> Lay bedded, changing oftentimes its form
> Like an uneasy snake: long time we sate,
> For scarcely more than one hour of the night,
> Such was our error, had been gone when we
> Renew'd our journey. On the rock we lay
> And wish'd to sleep but could not, for the stings
> Of insects, which with noise like that of noon
> Fill'd all the woods; the cry of unknown birds,
> The mountains, more by darkness visible
> And their own size, than any outward light,
> The breathless wilderness of clouds, the clock
> That told with unintelligible voice
> The widely-parted hours, the noise of streams
> And sometimes rustling motions nigh at hand
> Which did not leave us free from personal fear,
> And lastly the withdrawing Moon, that set
> Before us, while she still was high in heaven,
> These were our food, and such a summer's night
> Did to that pair of golden days succeed,
> With now and then a doze and snatch of sleep,
> On Como's Banks, the same delicious Lake.
>
> (631–57)

The poet advances into nature as a lover, accepts its difference from him, its sensuality, its immediacy, its irritability, its strangeness. All night long the lover turns to his beloved for her food, with only "now and then a doze and snatch of sleep." Into my expectations of Wordsworthian nature described as (maternal) idyllic ease or (paternal) serenity intrudes this excited scene of erotic immediacy producing epistemological confusion as pleasure.

Pleasure? I mean, in fact, something more intense, something that thrives on a confusion. (I think of Catullus' famous Lesbia poem, the second half of which begins: "Da mi basia mille" and describes the bliss of kisses as a willed confusion equal to erotic intensity, "conturbabimus.")[2] The word I'm looking for is bliss, or Barthes's *jouissance*. Pleasure, idyllic and peaceful, comes from control, from knowing the boundaries. Bliss comes from the breaking down of boundaries, of the known, and accepting, welcoming that condition. This the poet does at Lake Como.

Catullus asserts to his Lesbia that bliss challenges the "senex severiorum," the conventional wisdom of custom at which one hurls the imperturbable confusions of adolescent bliss. In the Como passage Wordsworth stretches the erotic and passionate to the larger dimensions of the French Revolution. An atmosphere of social upheaval seeps through the veil of nature: the Miltonic (Satanic) allusion to "darkness visible,"[3] the menacingly revolutionary and still sexual images of

> the sullen water underneath,
> On which a dull red image of the moon
> Lay bedded, changing oftentimes its form
> Like an uneasy snake. . . .

The imagination—in its *centripetal* capacity to unify, to control, to know —has no power here. It is barely desired. The imagination knows pleasure, but bliss surfaces at Lake Como. This is the other, *centrifugal* side of marriage.

This is a more troubling version of beauty, not marked by harmony, not marked by the domination of the imagination, curiously, not really a mountain scene, with its metaphorical implication that the mind dominates—stands above—physical reality. Instead beauty is confusion, epistemological uncertainty, yet animated by sexual and revolutionary imagery. Beauty is a language that wanders away from its subservience to that reality in order to call attention to itself.

Why does Wordsworth insert this scene here? I suspect he does not know (wonderfully, the poet does not write with his ideological imagination guiding him) but rather does not constrain the double impulse of his marriage to nature, of present Burkean ideology as well as past revolutionary urgency. Marriage as disappointment, as involving a substitution for the idealized object, seems to engender unexpected intensities. He has no solution (is it the pleasure of imagination at Simplon or the bliss of Como?) but admits the power of this moment and perhaps the taboo:

> But here I must break off, and quit at once,
> Though loth, the record of these wanderings,
> A theme which may seduce me else beyond
> All reasonable bounds.

A *Question about the Form*

of This Essay

Wordsworth breaks off, after the Como passage, perhaps the only point in *The Prelude* where imagination, reason in its most exalted mood, what de Man calls the "totalizing" impulse in Wordsworth, doesn't wrap things up. Depending on how one defines "Romantic," this might be the most Romantic moment in the poem. It remains open here, a fragment, containing within it an occasion for a seduction, an occasion not for pleasure but for passion or bliss. The fragment and the uncertainty invite me to enter the poetic moment to ask: why is this Lake Como passage here? Why would a poet, supremely sensitive both to danger and to bliss, supremely available to seduction, drawn inevitably to write about the loss of control and yet inevitably committed to writing about the recovery of control, break off?

I sense that the issue of passion, as a force to direct poetic activity— the use and the intention of language—would radically change the poem from what it presently is . . . if it were handled with less ambivalence and indirection—more positively, with less richness and texture. Wordsworth, I suspect, knows this but also knows that he could write such a poetry out of his personal and political experience and former, if not current, convictions. The fragment, the breaking off, allows him to write such knowledge into the poem but does not demand commitment to it.

And what of the openness of my essay on Romanticism and passion? Can I justify it to the extent that I can justify Wordsworth's breaking off? Says Paul de Man: "one is all too easily tempted to rationalize personal shortcoming as theoretical impossibility. . . ."[1] Have I capitulated to a Romantic form in a way that will make it impossible for me to develop any genuine critical distance on my subject? My form is an admission—that I do not have, historically speaking, a genuine critical distance on my subject, that I belong to Romanticism as much as I belong to an age trying to move beyond it. My form is an experiment—what will happen if I place myself within the formal assumptions of my subject and try, as in fact I have done autobiographically, to see my way beyond it, to establish my historical link to it not as a bondage but as a strength?

[34]
Holocaust and Poetic Language

For Wordsworth growth and consolation are one. Poetic language comes to him unbidden in moments of growth, and he summons it in moments of consolation. Usually one cannot easily separate the two functions of language, because growth—perceived always as an experience, even secondarily, of pleasure—always receives the confirming, connecting, reinforcing power of consolation. Language, appearing in this way, directs him not so much to thought, but to the signifier, the "music," the "feeling."

When he returned to Paris in 1792, "a little month" after the so-called September Massacres, burdened with the damaged hopes of the Revolutionary supporters, Wordsworth called on language to depoliticize this terrifying recent history pressing on his consciousness, to aestheticize it, to draw it and himself into the soothing river of English tradition. At least this is what the Burkean poet of *The Prelude* said he did. But the Burkean solution did not work here:

> I crossed (a black and empty area then)
> The Square of the Carousel, few weeks back
> Heap'd up with dead and dying, upon these
> And other sights looking as doth a man
> Upon a volume whose contents he knows
> Are memorable, but from him lock'd up,
> Being written in a tongue he cannot read,
> So that he questions the mute leaves with pain
> And half upbraids their silence.
>
> (X, 46–54)

He, like the witnesses of the Holocaust, cannot "read," control, the events. Like the night at Como, they remain a pressing, burdensome mystery. There may be a language to understand them, but it is foreign to him. The terror and sense of betrayal are more perverse in their mystery:

> The fear gone by
> Press'd on me almost like a fear to come;

[95]

I thought of those September Massacres,
Divided from me by a little month,
And felt and touch'd them, a substantial dread;
The rest was conjured up from tragic fictions,
And mournful calendars of true history,
Remembrances and dim admonishments.
'The horse is taught his manage, and the wind
Of heaven wheels round and treads in his own steps,
Year follows year, the tide returns again,
Day follows day, all things have second birth;
The earthquake is not satisfied at once.
And in such way I wrought upon myself,
Until I seem'd to hear a voice that cried,
To the whole City, 'Sleep no more.' To this
Add comments of a calmer mind, from which
I could not gather full security,
But at the best it seem'd a place of fear
Unfit for the repose of night which night requires,
Defenceless as a wood where tigers roam.

(X, 62–82)

The confrontation with holocaust where he expected to find liberty, equality, and fraternity turns the cherished sources of consolation—continuity with tradition, and poetic language—into a psychic shirt of Nessus. Tradition is the predictable recurrence of holocaust. Poetic language only reinforces the poet's implication in holocaust, his immobilizing guilt like that of Hamlet and Macbeth. This is one of the rare moments in Wordsworth where fantasy firmly molds perception and feeling, where all sorts of nonidyllic mental exertions and constructions, fantasies, obtrude upon the desire for consoling pleasure, where language and mind render him "Defenceless."

This is the moment, I think, that proves that the poet's experience of the French Revolution, his desire to overcome that experience, accounts for much of the autobiographical impulse of this poem. How can I recast my life so that in the majority of instances my appropriation of language will make me stronger, will heal me of the wounds of betrayal in the French Revolution? How can I show that my life, my strength is at the core apolitical? that politics and history and its disruptions are a cloud covering a moon, an appearance of change, but that the thing itself, the self, does not change except in the course of deepening from pleasure to pleasure?

Yet this passage, like the Lake Como episode, feels to be written in a language creating, for *The Prelude*, a different sense of beauty. One gropes for a way to describe the subtle change: it seems at once simpler, closer to the bone, to the reality of the event, to its pain, its fundamental confusion to the witnessing and participating person. Political, personal, and aesthetic intensities seem to press upon each other. The poet in no way loses control of his poetic function. Just as the poet surrounds himself with bad dreams, but dreams nevertheless, so language seems to take over, not harmonizing and allowing him to control his experience, but giving, from its own center of energy, its own shape to things.

"Klopstock"

We walked over to the window. It was still thundering in the distance, the blessed rain was falling on the land, and a most refreshing scent rose up to us with a rush of warm air. She stood there, leaning on her elbows, her gaze penetrating the countryside; she looked up at the sky, at me, and I could see tears in her eyes. She laid her hand on mine and said, "Klopstock." I knew at once of what she was thinking—his magnificent ode—and was lost in the emotions, that this one word aroused in me. I bent down and kissed her hand, and now there were tears in my eyes too as I looked into hers again. Oh, noble poet, if you could have seen the adoration in those eyes! I hope I need never have to hear your name, so oft profaned, spoken again by any other lips! [1]

The name of the popular Sturm und Drang poet seals Werther's bliss in the moment, which is flooded with sensations. Klopstock wrote a rites-of-spring ode, more Ossianic than Chaucerian—that is, the sensations immediately get channeled into fantasy and longing. Who knows where Lotte is?—A woman of the gaze and yet it is not a man's sublime gaze; it takes in everything including Werther, but it does not control or distance. Instead it releases her tears, and, in a significantly feminine gesture, her touch. "Klopstock," too, seems part of an immediacy of experience, part of a self-absorption (Lotte *reads only what confirms* her sense of herself) that is also an intimate communication.

"Klopstock," coming from Lotte, makes Werther dissolve. Often she puts him in a full confusion: he does not know where he is; he sees nothing but her; he has no self; he yields to this state without resistance, as in a sexual bliss. But in his report of the moment, here, he garners at least as much affection for the poet as for the woman. "Klopstock" has united them; he knows it; and he "catches fire" for the poet, the poem. Immediately he becomes possessive and concentrates on her purity, his adoration (the gaze), and returns to himself.

To the "modern reader" this passage probably occasions a snicker. Not only do we see it as a species of sentimentality, but probably the word "Klopstock" sounds like a bit of Romantic jargon. It has the imprecision of jargon that conflates several precise designations: "Klopstock" signifies an author; but also the "spirit" of an author—that disembodied purity of poetic inspiration, the genius; the magnificent ode that he wrote; the landscape (before their streaming eyes) that recalls the landscapes of the poem; and the feelings they are encountering in themselves. Finally, it is a (not so secret) code that enjoins Lotte and Werther to the same cult of feeling, a cult that stands—at least in this instant—outside the worldview and familiarity of the dominant social order. It is an instrument, a technology.

"Klopstock" enacts a drama of the Sublime. Through the immediacy of touch and mutual understanding it stimulates desire and fantasy, the dissolution of order, the courting of sexual pleasure, the fulfillment of the body, pleasure in the companion, and the excitement of the mind encrusted with the jewels of wish and thought. But the Word is not the thing itself; the word in relation to the experience of love is finally chaste, and Werther seizes upon this chasteness and adores it. All the diffuse pleasure funnels into mind and subjectivity, which for the moment is enough.

The Romantic Word occasions only a tenuous connection between people. The mutuality or commonality it assumes and demands cannot withstand the range of human feelings, the recognition of which means the acceptance of the differences between persons. There may be a connection between Werther's adoration of this Romantic poetic language and his wrestling with an aggressivity that is either ineffectual (his attempted defense of the peasant who killed the new lover of the widow he loved) or self-annihilating. Interestingly, he kills himself in the presence of another very popular work, Lessing's tragedy of passion-love, *Emilia Galotti*.

I think that the young Goethe understood brilliantly the crippling psychological and social insufficiencies of the Sublime. Werther's actual death and the passions aroused in others by both his life and his death overwhelm the fantasies of the complacent solitude of domination that the Sublime engenders. Coleridge reverts to the conservative hope for the Sublime Word in his domestic poem "This Lime-Tree Bower My Prison" when he tries through poetry to wed himself to his urban friend Charles Lamb:

> My gentle-hearted Charles! when the last rook
> Beat its straight path along the dusky air
> Homewards, I blest it! deeming its black wing
> (Now a dim speck, now vanishing in light)
> Had cross'd the mighty Orb's dilated glory,
> While thou stood'st gazing; or, when all was still,

> Flew creeking o'er thy head, and had a charm
> For thee, my gentle-hearted Charles, to whom
> No sound is dissonant which tells of Life.

Lamb wrote Coleridge that he hated the epithet "gentle-hearted" because, as he said, "I hope that my virtues have done sucking."[2] The rook, fixed in a transcendent image, instead of freely bringing Coleridge and Lamb into intimacy, felt to the latter like an intrusion upon his own freedom and upon the truth about his character and values; apparently it felt like an infantilization. What appears to have been intended as love turned out to have the effect of aggression. What appears as a gesture of openness and vulnerability, of intimacy, turns out to mask some wish for domination in solitude.

Byron's "To the Po" absorbs the assumptions of the power of the Romantic Word only to elaborate, painfully, its inadequate accounting for the passions of love. Returning, line after line, to the idea that the water in the river he now looks at will soon be seen by her whom he loves, Byron cannot rest in this observation as proof or occasion for intimacy. The reason for their permanent separateness resides elsewhere, in his fear of passion, his passion to resist passion. The poem records his enslavement by passion; the Romantic Word stands above it. The intimacy which the imagination can picture ("Klopstock," the rook, the Po) belongs to an idyll of beauty, a moment of calm without desire, that stands at a remove from Lord Byron.

> I have struggled long
> To love again no more as I once loved.
> Oh! Time! why leave this earliest Passion strong?
> To tear a heart which pants to be unmoved?

[36]
"Either . . . Or"

You say that I must "either" have hope of winning Lotte "or" I must have none. Very well. In the first case I am to try to grasp the fulfillment of my wish and make my hopes come true; in the second I am to pull myself together and try to rid myself of this miserable emotion that must in the end utterly debilitate me.[1]

"Either . . . or" refers to the attempt "either" to realize "or" to suppress the drives. In the eighteenth-century novel this usually means challenging or accepting the rules of a domestic social order. In either instance the person makes a choice and acts upon it.

But Werther offers a third possibility, since the first two risk either too much or too little: to remain in and create an atmosphere of adultery but ascribe to oneself an illness that renders him in his chosen situation helpless, passive, defective:

can you demand of an unfortunate human who is dying by inches of an insidious disease that he should end his misery with one knife thrust? Wouldn't you rather say that his misfortune weakens him to such an extent that it must rob him also of the courage to rid himself of it?[2]

For Werther the insidious disease is precisely what is best about him, the availability of his "soul" to another—Lotte's "soul." That communion refuses to acknowledge, except negatively, the society that rejects it. To commit suicide would not merely bring an end to suffering but would end the communion.

Later on Werther kills himself anyway. Suicide done in despair and without any particular courage has accumulated the meaning of a deepened communion with the beloved.

"Either . . . or" in Werther (1774) is situated within the critique of domesticity and monogamy. The refusal to choose between the two possibilities occurs through a subtle but characteristic shift from the traditional assumption that a person's worth is equated with the quality and effect of his willed actions to a Romantic assumption that the moral and social judgment made upon a person must be mediated through a judgment upon his health. This new preoccupation with the inner life concerns not simply the life of the individual but a self-sufficient inner world that can be easily bruised by the social world but is supposed to draw its strength and confirmation from other similarly directed selves. This is the world of the sentiment of existence.

Goethe displays the skepticism of the Romantic liberal about the possible self-sufficiency of the modern person; clearly Werther has an effect and is effected by others who are persuaded by the contemporary social ethos. But Wordsworth, in what Marilyn Butler has called a counterrevolutionary decade,[3] removes this skepticism. "The Solitary Reaper" (1805) turns "either . . . or" into mental play. That poem, while it withdraws powerfully from the outer world, while it reduces its field and dissolves the social world in the lake of the mind, nonetheless produces a comedy of mental life. If it is a world of outer scarcity, it creates a world of inner plenitude:

> Will no one tell me what she sings?—
> Perhaps the plaintive numbers flow
> For old, unhappy, far-off things,
> And battles long ago:
> Or is it some more humble lay,
> Familiar matter of to-day?
> Some natural sorrow, loss, or pain,
> That has been, and may be again?
>
> Whate'er the theme, the Maiden sang
> As if her song could have no ending;
> I saw her singing at her work,
> And o'er the sickle bending;—
> I listened, motionless and still;
> And, as I mounted up the hill,—
> The music in my heart I bore,
> Long after it was heard no more.

In recent American Romantics studies, "The Solitary Reaper" has had an unusually powerful influence. Geoffrey Hartman, whose beautiful reading (1964) made it newly interesting, affirmed it as a poem of inner plenitude—of multiple moods, fluidities, doublings, expansions, "a sustained inner freedom in the face of death, disbelief, and fact."[4] This last suggests that play and mental freedom constitute a resistance: the inner world—like Rousseau's in his gently rocking boat far from history—is perceived as challenging and challenged by an outer one (defined by Hartman—and Romantics from Rousseau and Schiller on—with reference not to history and society but to eternal matters like death and spirit).

The resistance appears as a drastic reduction in conscious, self-conscious, critical, and generally intersubjective mental activity along with a corresponding increase in an aestheticizing and transcendentalizing of the immediate world. The poem, however, starts out as a dramatic monologue in which the voice projects its own immediacy and vulnerability into the singing and reaping girl. At the beginning of the poem she seems so near and available that he must consider her response to or interruption by unwary travelers. He could approach her, engage her. But by the end the presumed immediacy, the emergent possibility turns out to have been a quotation from the past; instead the poem is another instance of Wordsworthian autobiography. The self that writes the poem has walked out of the theater of vulnerability. Time has "matured" him, and the occasion for his entering into the woman's history, for her becoming visible and known to him, has vanished with time. She leaves history and enters art; he drops the cry of uncertainty and desire and the disruption of the risk of renewed life and becomes the autobiographer who confirms the unbroken identity of past and present.

The luxury of "either . . . or" grammars in Romantic writing lies, finally, in the fact that one feels no need to make a choice between the alternatives. As a result, the mind reverts to its own pleasure in producing signifiers.

Conversion

Just as Romantic autobiography can be viewed as a reactive and defensive phenomenon or a product of ideology, so the Romantic encounter with nature does not refer to the purity of that encounter. Nature, both before and after Romanticism, is the embodiment of danger and uncertainty and indifference; it is that from which we must protect ourselves. Nature in Romanticism is converted, through the bourgeois capitalist fantasy of the possibility of acquiring happiness and the beautiful and the good, from the unconstrained and the indifferent into that which can be bought and thus controlled. We dominate the land which in turn gives us the gift of happiness.

The melancholy undercurrent of much Romantic meditative poetry, observes Raymond Williams, results from rendering the other—whether the laborer or the feminine—invisible or disenfranchised: the subject is lonely (and possibly guilty). To prevent or at least counter the loneliness, the writer may convert—through his imagination and his art—the depopulated, dead landscape into one populated by the "society" of nature. Enraged by his "enemies" in society, Rousseau turns to the natural world in solitude:

> The deeper the solitude that surrounds me, the greater the need I feel at such times for something to fill the vacuum, and where my imagination cannot provide me with ideas or my memory rejects them, the earth makes up for this with the many objects which it produces spontaneously, without any human agency, and sets before my eyes on all sides.[1]

It is precisely the "spontaneity" of persons who think differently from him that Rousseau has come to fear, so he personifies nature as spontaneous. Wordsworth's "bliss of solitude" is another such conversion—"bliss," because, instead of *dancing with people,* the poet, or rather his "heart" (the organ of the sentiment of existence and a telling metonymy), "dances with the daffodils."

[38]

The Isolate Feminine Voice

In a note to *Maria* (1797) Mary Wollstonecraft sketches a dramatic and prophetic ending to the novel she did not live to complete: "The conflict is over!" says Maria, "I will live for my child!" [1] Her child is a daughter; the conflict involves suicide as a solution to the attacks from men on her life and on the typical radical articulation of a suffocating life for women. This is only one of the several "hints," as her editor-widower Godwin calls them, of how the novel might have concluded. A powerful feminist solution to the problems of patriarchy lives only as a small voice in a footnote.

On the final plate of *Visions of the Daughters of Albion* (1793) by Wollstonecraft's radical sympathizer William Blake, Oothoon—raped by a tyrannical masculine principle responding to her independent sexual energies— concludes her lengthy song with the Blakean motto: "every thing that lives is *holy*!" The illustration below that text depicts Oothoon as prophetess flying through dark flaming stormclouds over the ocean, arms and hair outstretched, eyes intensely piercing straight into the reader's gaze. Some daughters of Albion huddling on the shore look up as she passes (not noticing them) overhead. Strangely, they hear her song as "woes" and "eccho back her sighs."

The vision of the wronged woman who attempts to discern the system of oppression goes unheard or is easily misinterpreted.

39

The Halted Traveler before

the Art Object

Eighteenth-century lyric poetry and particularly that of Wordsworth sometimes represents a person arrested by a sight or sound emanating from the natural world. Sometimes an epitaphic voice (*"sta viator"*) calls on the traveler to halt and listen to a message from the other world; sometimes the traveler himself stops and is penetrated by a message or vision. Geoffrey Hartman, who has caused readers to halt before such poems, sees the moment as muted apocalypse often in the form of lyric admonition in a melancholy or mournful affect.

Why would the poems of Wordsworth have struck an audience as radical? The "language of real men" discussion is only part of the answer and may—as many have said—finally be specious. But some of his poems enact a discovery of a vision of pleasure and power. I posit that the Wordsworthian traveler before he is halted wanders in a kind of preconscious haze ("lonely as a cloud"), no longer susceptible to a radical consciousness but still very vulnerable to the lure of "possible worlds." Schiller would say he lives in a state of "filled infinity." The daffodils or the solitary reaper focuses and limits that state with something from reality at the same time they grant excitability and plenitude to the inner life.

Does this mean that the poet ritualizes the preference for inner over outer life? My guess is that in the first decade of the nineteenth century these poems did not have that effect, but to the degree that people thought about them at all, they saw the possibility that for the bourgeois individual, lost and dulled in a hazy, alienating ignorance, the visions of utter beauty penetrating consciousness in the midst of one's "endless way" would enliven a person into a new (potentially critical) connection with his world. Thus "the bliss of solitude" or the "music in my heart" may have initiated a feeling of genuine excitement. "Bliss," after all (as Barthes talks about it) is a destabilizing condition. The "bliss of solitude" may overwhelm the assumption that solitude means idyllic ease, private peace, where the boundaries of mind and body fully contain the pleasure. Is this why reviewers of "Moods of My Own Mind" in the 1807 *Poems, in Two Volumes* condemned these "private" lyrics as "trivial" and, worst of all, "effiminate"? and why, ten years later, they condemned for essentially the same reasons Keats's early excursions in sensual fantasy and language?

In 1807 the literary traveler may have halted before an admonishing voice proclaiming bliss, a voice more radical than one reminding the unaware person of his "mortality."

40

Wollstonecraft's Animadversion on
Rousseau's Sensibility

But all Rousseau's errors in reasoning arose from sensibility, and sensibility to their charms women are very ready to forgive!

Sensibility, says Mary Wollstonecraft, meets in man and woman as a conspiracy to keep women powerless.

When he should have reasoned he became impassioned, and reflection inflamed his imagination instead of enlightening his understanding. Even his virtues also led him further astray; for, born with a warm constitution and lively fancy, nature carried him toward the other sex with such eager fondness, that he soon becam lascivious. Had he given way to these desires, the fire would have extinguished itself in a natural manner; but virtue, and a romantic kind of delicacy, made him practice self-denial; yet, when fear, delicacy, or virtue, restrained him, he debauched his imagination, and reflecting on the sensations to which fancy gave force, he traced them in the most glowing colours, and sunk them deep into his soul.[1]

I am reminded of John Gilbert Cooper's 1755 assessment of Collins' quintessential poem of reflection, the "Ode to Evening," which he says "warms the breast with a sympathetic Glow of retired Thoughtfulness."[2] The poet cathects not the world but rather his own mind-in-reflection. Cooper admires this in Collins; Wollstonecraft criticizes it in Rousseau because it produces his retrograde vision of woman educated toward dependence upon and support of the *patriarch*.

One thinks of Blake:

> What is it men in women do require?—
> The lineaments of Gratified Desire.
> What is it women do in men require?—
> The lineaments of Gratified Desire.[3]

Rousseau's refusal to gratify desire engenders sensibility, a mixture of lust and prudishness and "depth of soul," in Blake's mythology, Enitharmon's and Orc's hunger of moans and possessive violence.

"Feminine" persons are duped and confused by the language of such self-preoccupation:

> they imagine that their understanding is convinced when they only sympathize with a poetic writer, who skilfully exhibits the objects of sense, most voluptuously shadowed or gracefully veiled—And thus making us feel whilst dreaming that we reason, erroneous conclusions are left in the mind.[4]

Is this a radical, feminist critique of Romantic poetic language? Does Wollstonecraft's negative "shadowed" and "veiled" correspond to Wordsworth's positive "colouring" of imagination? How much does the reality of the dream necessarily refuse (by obscuring) the reality of the object? She exposes the limitations of feeling as an instrument of knowledge: it confuses dreaming with reasoning, producing a mild and socially acceptable psychosis that, however, will not allow genuine difference.

In a question that exactly formulates the emotional range and extravagance of sensibility, she asks:

> Why was Rousseau's life divided between ecstasy and misery? Can any other answer be given than this, that the effervescence of his imagination produced both; but, had his fancy been allowed to cool, it is possible that he might have acquired more strength of mind.[5]

The inner life has become too "voluptuous," too compelling. The reality of the other, she implies, tempers and focuses and balances the innate recklessness of emotion left to itself. Rousseau's is the emotion of grandiosity, which translates socially and politically into the assertion of male domination. (N.B.:Beauty, following Rousseau, fills the space controlled by grandiosity, in which desire, constrained by love of self, and weak in relation to "the other," would vanish.)

How brilliantly she refutes Rousseau's labored distinction, in his confessional writings, between the self, untouchable and untaintable by society and definitively innocent, and the self whose actions have effects and who can be acted upon and inevitably diminished by society! Her analysis of his mental life which otherwise belongs merely to him serves to explain the sources of his sexism: the private self and the public, authorial self are finally one. *Amour de soi* dissolves into *amour propre*. Or rather, there is only one *amour* and it always has some effect beyond the one who feels it. Wollstonecraft concludes: "I war only with the sensibility that led him to degrade woman by making her the slave of love."[6]

41

Charles Lamb's Rosamund Gray

Historically *Rosamund Gray*[1] (1798), like *Paul et Virginie*, enacts (typically in the late eighteenth century) the self-destruction of natural passional urges. Biographically, it seems to be Lamb's primary effort in literature to dramatize the inner experience of his sister Mary's murder of their mother with a knife just two years before and to effect some psychological distance from that traumatic event. Generically it may open the door for the eventual emergence of one of England's premier familiar essayists.

Rosamund Gray struggles to free herself from the bondage of piety and imposed duty. Having lost her parents (who perhaps could have made her struggle far less severe), she lives with a blind and infirm grandmother, fully dependent upon the girl and unconsciously feeding that dependency. When Rosamund tries to climb out of a window, daringly, onto the limb of an old tree, she slips and falls. When Rosamund has given herself fully to drawing a larger picture than ever before, probably in order to give her artwork to the young man she loves, the old lady in her physical but not psychological blindness destroys it by throwing it away. Allan Clare is in love with her. As Rosamund's drive toward her own satisfaction mounts, Allan Clare's love for her mounts also. His sister Elinor befriends Rosamund, leading her beyond the orbit of grandmaternal tyranny. (Significantly, the sister is ten years older than Allan, just as Mary Lamb—the impassioned murderer— was ten years older than Charles.) One evening, unable to sleep, feeling the pull of the natural world, Rosamund stealthily leaves her infirm charge and wanders into the night. Alone, the grandmother awakens in a panic of mortality, drags herself to Rosamund's bed, and dies, with a smile (blessed or satanic—it's not clear) on her face. Simultaneously, Rosamund encounters a cold, vengeful (Godwinian?) man, with a disembodied single name, Matravis, and is raped. She manages to find her way to the Clares where she soon dies. Sometime later Elinor dies too.

So much, it seems, for the desires and the lives of women.

The story now cuts to a later time. The narrator, after growing up in the big city and entering the profession of medicine as a surgeon, returns to the village of his boyhood, the village of the above story. Trying through imagination to recover the atmosphere of his childhood, he happens to encounter Allan Clare, now a wandering, sweetly melancholy, and celibate figure. The two become fast friends. Clare says to the narrator:

> The melancholy, which comes over me with the recollection of [those early events], is not hurtful, but only tends to soften and tranquilise my mind, to detach me from the restlessness of human pursuits.
>
> The stronger I feel this detachment, the more I find myself drawn heavenward to the contemplation of spiritual objects.[2]

That is, as time passes, he separates himself from passion and draws nearer to the cool unconnectedness, the "disinterestedness" of spirit. He calls himself a wanderer and sounds like a version of his contemporary, the naturebound, autodidact pedlar of *The Ruined Cottage*.

Clare returns with the surgeon-narrator to the city where the former takes pleasure in visiting the sick to offer a bit of consolation.

This brief novel ends when the two visit the bedside of the dying Matravis. Matravis dies delirious, with the narrator and Clare incapable of identifying themselves to him, incapable of granting the evil figure any final peace.

The story is first about the eradication of the feminine—not so much as a principle but simply as a presence. Rosamund, her grandmother, her mother, her sororal friend Elinor, in effect three generations, *all* women die. Even the perverted feminine presences (the grandmother and maybe even Matravis—is *mater* in his name?) have no opportunity to convert their negativity into something life-giving. The tragedy of the story, beyond the death of Rosamund, is the silencing of the feminine. This is a world without female love, more simply, impoverished of half the race. What survives and seems likely to thrive is the masculine bond, the narrator and Clare.

They base their fraternity first on their distance from a traumatic past which they, to greater or lesser degree, share, and second on their penchant for healing. They need to hold that past, with its disruptive dramas of the feminine, at a distance. And that distance is proportional to the healing process. Can they, as male comrades, recover some of the feminine as nurturance? Interestingly, they have no power to reach or touch the dying Matravis. Yet they are not overcome by him. Lamb seems to want to show that their distance from the original event and their curative instincts and skills are not all-powerful, but conversely that the event cannot swamp them.

One can begin to predict Lamb the essayist from *Rosamund Gray*. He appears displaced onto Clare and the surgeon-narrator. Clare can tell a story sympathetically. He has an instinct for spiritual healing. The surgeon has honed the art of not telling but writing tales from the past, not professionally but casually. He is quite literally an amateur. Like Lamb the essayist he reenters the actual rooms of childhood in an effort to reacquaint the present with the benign energy of early life. Assuming that each character in the story comprises some aspect of Lamb himself, one can say that the surgeon has neutralized and sublimated his aggressive feelings through the art of "healing."

A comparison with Wordsworth's contemporary *The Ruined Cottage* suggests that the drama of facing and surviving extravagant, passionate, potentially subversive human experience must have been highly compelling in the 1790s. Knowing the biographies of both Lamb and Wordsworth, I can sense a powerful identification with the person burdened with extravagant passions. Ordinarily one might wish to associate this identification with the elegiac paradigm, but it is more important to make the further connection to the burdens of contemporary revolutionary consciousness. Wordsworth, I think, is much more severe with that consciousness than is Lamb, because the former utterly seals over any indignation or rage at the social conditions that produced the disruption of Margaret's home life, her derangement and death. He refuses to see the political resonance in this instance of the silencing of the feminine. For Lamb the experience of Matravis' bad acts, the rawness of his deranged, unrepentent state remains vividly intractable, recalcitrant.

Unlike Wordsworth, who with *The Ruined Cottage* becomes the Romantic poet of consolation, Lamb turns (ambivalently, to be sure) to cultural criticism in a form—the familiar essay—that only ambivalently catches its power from the early Romantic poem, the genre of consolation. I find it moving and symbolically precise that William Hazlitt, in his brilliant piece of cultural criticism of Wordsworth and Coleridge, "My First Acquaintance with Poets," concludes with a dismissal of the poets and a welcoming of the essayist Lamb as a friend:

> It was at Godwin's that I met [Lamb] with Holcroft and Coleridge, where they were disputing fiercely which was the best—*Man as he was, or man as he is to be*. "Give me," says Lamb, "man as he is *not* to be." This saying was the beginning of a friendship between us, which I believe still continues. — [3]

Could Lamb have sensed, when he eschewed the writing of poetry after the family disaster, that the major currents of contemporary poetry would not contain or honor the truth of such intense passions? that contemporary poetry (e.g., Wordsworth) would not entertain the possibility that the honesty of pain, of irreconciliation, might be more liberating than pleasure? If the answer is yes, it would go a way toward explaining his friendship with Hazlitt.

42

Disappointment

.

"From the part Mr. Burke took in the American Revolution, it was natural that I should consider him friend to mankind," said Tom Paine in the opening sentence of *The Rights of Man*.[1] "I am astonished and disappointed. . . ." Similarly, notes James Chandler, Wordsworth was disappointed when Richard Watson (bishop of Llandaff) turned against the French people after having given support to the Colonies during the American Revolution.[2] Thirty years later William Hazlitt's "My First Acquaintance with Poets" (1823), "On Going a Journey" (1821),[3] and other essays obsessively record *his* disappointment with Wordsworth, Coleridge, and Southey for their "apostasy," their rejection of radical causes and their embrace of the established government and the "brand of JUS DIVINUM." Romantic radical sentiment, from the beginning to the end of the period, springs from disappointment at betrayals by radical leaders and heroes.

Hazlitt sees disappointment everywhere: it is his burden and genius as social and cultural critic of the Regency period and the subsequent ten years to turn "disappointment" into an instrument of analysis and evaluation of his age. Disappointment describes for him the career of his father, a dissenting minister relegated to the periphery of public life, ending his days dreaming out his battles for justice and reform by pouring over biblical texts.

> So if we look back to past generations (as far as the eye can reach) we
> see the same hopes, fears, wishes, followed by the same disappointments, throbbing in the human heart; and so we may see them (if
> we look forward) rising up for ever, and disappearing, like vapourish
> bubbles, in the human breast![4]

The Romantic imagination, he implies, *is a consequence of disappointment.*

Elsewhere he speculates, stunningly, on Wordsworth's career and poetics as a function of the post-Revolutionary "disappointment machine":

> Possibly a good deal of this [Wordsworth's subjectivity in poetry and
> his ascetic strain] may be regarded as the effect of disappointed views

and an inverted ambition. Prevented by native pride and indolence from climbing the ascent of learning or greatness, taught by political opinions to say to the vain pomp and glory of the world, "I hate ye," seeing the path of classical and artificial poetry blocked up by the cumbrous ornaments of style and turgid *commonplaces,* so that nothing more could be achieved in that direction but by the most ridiculous bombast or the tamest servility; he has turned back partly from the bias of his mind, partly perhaps from a judicious policy—has struck into the sequestered vale of humble life, sought out the Muse among sheepcotes and hamlets and the peasant's mountain-haunts, has discarded all the tinsel pageantry of verse, and endeavoured (not in vain) to aggrandise the trivial and add the charm of novelty to the familiar.[5]

A faintly Dantesque topography runs through Hazlitt's analysis: blocked from ascending the mountain of learning and greatness by the ferocious animals, pride and indolence, Wordsworth turns back, and down, to the "other way" of rural life and trivial and familiar objects. This underworld, or sequestered vale, emits that kind of ambiguity that often follows disappointment: weakness and escape on the one hand and, on the other, the vital confrontation with one's own character, an assessment of the inner and outer truth of the moment. The sequestered vale of rural life becomes Dante's— and all heroes'—*via negativa;*[6] and yet, Hazlitt implies elsewhere, Wordsworth seems to have settled permanently into what ought to have been a path on the way to—at the very least—the city of a new humanity. Making his home in the negative way has turned him into an egotist, a poet wedded to illusions and committed in his poetry to perpetrating them and to fashioning an audience rarified enough to assent to them.

Hazlitt's great gift as a cultural critic is a capacity to identify with the themes of the Romantic movement, to know them firsthand, and at the same time to turn those themes into instruments of his own cultural criticism. Perhaps Romanticism, as an early-nineteenth-century phenomenon, begins to dissolve when Hazlitt exposes the power that "disappointment" holds over contemporary writers. In this sense Hazlitt's most telling piece of Romantic criticism is "On Going a Journey" (1821), a meditation on a favorite Romantic activity, walking, an activity that situates so many Romantic poems and attitudes (going back to Werther and Rousseau). Coleridge, he nostalgically and enviously claims in the essay, could walk and talk at the same time, "could go on in the most delightful explanatory way over hill and dale, a summer's day, and convert a landscape into a didactic poem or a Pindaric ode. . . . If I could so clothe my ideas in sounding and flowing words, I might perhaps wish to have someone with me to admire the swelling theme. . . ."[7] There was a prophetic, visionary, hopeful, defiant quality in the Coleridge and Wordsworth of 1798, a quality with which Hazlitt—at age twenty—felt fully identified. The disappointment in their change runs deep, resurfacing two or three times in this essay. But Hazlitt's essay does not by any means rest in his disappointment. Rather, he wonders if his disappointment rests upon a misconception of poetic value and effectuality, a misconception held by Wordsworth and Coleridge and bought wholesale by himself.

In the above passage Hazlitt mimics the Wordsworthian language of throwing a coloring of imagination, like a cloak, over objects. Instead of seeing this activity as a way of making familiar objects unfamiliar, thus bringing them to attention, Hazlitt sees it as obfuscation, the willful creation of confusion and mystification. Sound is valued over sense; recalling Wordsworth and Coleridge twenty-three years after the famous meeting with them, Hazlitt describes the sound of their voices rather than the content of their verses.

He further correlates mystification of objects and ideas with an inflated notion of the power of the imagination to bring all sorts of objects and ideas under a single umbrella of disinterestedness. This, Hazlitt believes, is a grandiose fantasy of the power of the imagination, "egotism," and in a more sinister sense, a wish for domination and excessive control. Hazlitt lightly but brilliantly ushers his critique of imagination into a critique of the Romantic walk:

> There is hardly any thing that shows the short-sightedness or capriciousness of the imagination more than travelling does. With change of place we change our ideas; nay, our opinions and feelings. We can by an effort indeed transport ourselves to old and long-forgotten scenes, and then the picture of the mind revives again; but we forget those that we have just left. It seems that we can think but of one place at a time. The canvas of the fancy has only a certain extent, and if we paint one set of objects upon it, they immediately efface every other. We cannot enlarge our conceptions; we only shift our point of view. . . . The world in our conceit of it is not much bigger than a nutshell. It is not one prospect expanded into another, county joined to county, kingdom to kingdom, lands to seas, making an image voluminous and vast. . . . In trying to renew old recollections, we cannot as it were

unfold the whole web of our existence; we must pick out the single threads.[8]

So Hazlitt, doing a manner of self-analysis, quits the Romantic imagination of his youth, not to deny it but, again, to try to understand it. He picks out the moment that led to his disappointment:

> I could stand on some tall rock, and overlook the precipice of years that separates me from what I then was. I was at that time going shortly to visit the poet whom I have above named [Coleridge]. Where is he now? Not only I myself have changed; the world, which was then new to me, has become old and incorrigible. Yet I will turn to thee in thought, O sylvan Dee, as then thou wert, in joy, in youth and gladness; and thou shalt always be to me the river of Paradise, where I will drink of the waters of life freely![9]

Both psychologically and ideologically, Hazlitt wants to retain the life-and-hope-giving powers of imagination (see the Wordsworth allusions in the above lines) but not to be imprisoned or deluded by them. It is a difficult, an anguishing, task and always has been since Hazlitt, for the cultural critic. But at the core of it, for Hazlitt, lay the conviction that an aesthetic based upon disappointment would not support a truly progressive political program.

43

Demystifying Romanticism:

A Diary Entry

I am guided in this essay on Romanticism by a simple belief, based on perceptions and readings and—above all—convictions, that we need today to demystify Romanticism. Demystification is really the critique not so much of a historical period as of a present-day corruption in the use to which we put art—a corruption fostering sentimentality in us and encouraging that beauty and social or personal reality be kept separate, that the purity of the beautiful requires the bad present.

But then I open Rilke's *Letters on Cézanne* and see:

> As if these colors could heal one of indecision once and for all. The good conscience of these reds, these blues, their simple truthfulness, it educates you; and if you stand beneath them as acceptingly as possible, it's as if they were doing something for you.[1]

And I think: Romantic poetry is so often the art of healing; not only did the poets intend this, but in fact it so easily does heal. It's a poetry of integration of self. It's a poetry that seeks to incorporate the feminine into its structures of masculine assertiveness and anxiety. It points the reader toward a fullness and an acceptance of the competing elements in his inner life. A poem like the "Intimations Ode" serves as both model and experience for the reader who will "stand beneath it as acceptingly as possible." This poem, and so many other Romantic lyrics, whatever their political colorings, encourage the widening and deepening of the inner life, of the self, encourage a generosity toward oneself which leads—I think—to greater generosity toward others. Would I, I wonder, be more generous in my reading of these poems, more generous and accepting of their rhetoric and intentions, if I accepted them more generously?

But then, if I would learn to accept, through Romantic poetry, more of myself, I would have to accept the skeptical side as well: those perceptions and convictions that are not content to merge fully with the Romantic intention and with the use to which post-Romantic readers have put Romanticism.

The fact is that, although I may privately experience the art of the past in an unmediated way from time to time and—in that special condition of reading, *teaching*—try to encourage the unmediated response in students as the ground of our exploration, I want to write (and teach) finally as a late-twentieth-century American, for whom the artifacts of the past shimmer in the powerful, unsettling light of recent cultural assumptions and social experiences. Trilling said that Keats's urn—standing for the old cultural artifact—consoles us (i.e., lets us simplify our response) as a friendly image of wholeness because "pastness is one of its attributes."[2] We are not, I take it, supposed to question the past or the present's assumptions about it. In another place Trilling similarly speaks of Wordsworth's leech gatherer as a "Paraclete," that is, a figure pointing toward a realization and a transformation.[3] Here is the possibility for a more lively experience within the reading subject. But the artifact, while it lives (in Trilling's view) for the spiritual transformation of the reader, must remain untouched by a historical imagination insofar as it is a skeptical or critical one.

44

Crystallization

Everything can be acquired in solitude, except character.
—Stendhal, *De l'amour*

Many readings of Romantic literature, whether from the political right or from the left, fail to satisfy finally because they forget the *true* nature of fantasy: that it *usually* implies recognition of another subject, another, in the real world. The fundamental domesticated interpretation of Romantic literature is that the representation of fantasy implies the subject's absorption in himself, his negation of anything or anyone beyond himself except as an object of *use* or as an object of *worship*. In this view lies a terribly naive and destructive assumption about the experience of communication between two people: that the conduit between them is clear, without resistance, that if the conduit is textured with the internal life of the subject, that subject has relinquished interest in or capacity for the other person. This truly is an idyllic fantasy to which, unfortunately, some feminist readers have recently submitted. Specifically, they say that male representations of masculine erotic fantasy persist in turning the woman into a static object. I argue the opposite—that that representation usually signals the recognition of the mobility or subjecthood of the woman-as-feminine and calls for the kind of psychic and possibly social destabilization that feminism usually advocates. The most elaborate and ingenious contemporary work on the subject is Stendhal's *De l'amour* (1821); its value extends far beyond its idiosyncrasies, for it theorizes upon a major preoccupation in European literature for the previous half-century. And it is no accident that *De l'amour* appeared within only two years of Keats's love letters and poems to Fanny Brawne, Shelley's *Epipsychidion*, Byron's *Don Juan*, and Hazlitt's *Liber Amoris*. Unlike all the above except Byron's *Don Juan*, *De l'amour* releases a *comic* energy.

Stendhal turns most directly to the subject I raise in his section "Werther and Don Juan." "[Don Juan's relationship with] women kills every other enjoyment in life: Werther's way increases them a hundredfold."[1] Don Juan's love is an emotion of the same kind as a love of hunting."[2] Love à la Werther "is a fresh aim in life with which everything is connected. . . . Everything is alive, and everything breathes the most passionate interest."[3]

De l'amour is about love à la Werther, and contains within it a vision of women liberated, through education and meaningful work, toward happiness. Although it is not a politically radical book, *De l'amour* bears significant similarities, in this regard, to Mary Wollstonecraft's *Vindication* and *Maria*.

Happiness grows out of the complex, highly textured and changeable passions and fantasy life of man and woman toward each other. The *intenser, the realer* that other person becomes, the more the thickness of fantasy and ancient personal expectation fills the conduit. The sweetness and excitement of love are the fine residuum of self-preoccupations heightened and opened toward the beloved. Primarily the reality of the beloved stimulates the fantasy life (except in truly neurotic cases, which Romantic poets do not usually write about). For these reasons Simone de Beauvoir can write: "Stendhal is at the same time deeply romantic and decidedly a feminist. . . . It is not only in the name of Freedom in general, it is in the name of individual happiness that Stendhal demands the emancipation of women."[4]

"Crystallization" is Stendhal's famous metaphor for the experience of love:

> Leave a lover with his thoughts for twenty-four hours, and this is what will happen:
>
> At the salt mines of Salzburg, they throw a leafless wintery bough into one of the abandoned workings. Two or three months later they pull it out covered with a shining deposit of crystals. The smallest twig, no bigger than a tom-tit's claw, is studded with a galaxy of scintillating diamonds. The original branch is no longer recognizable.
>
> What I have called crystallization is a mental process which draws from everything that happens new proofs of the perfection of the loved one.[5]

Immediately the view of the beloved becomes subject to the fantasy of perfection, or "perfect" beauty. As soon as desire for the other makes itself known, it becomes desire for something, in a sense, larger than the beloved and more intimate. Only in one way is it less "real": love emerges from precisely the magnitude (though not necessarily the distortion) of the illusory experience. The passion for the real person gets expressed through the illusion. This creates both the happiness and the torture of the early stages of love. It also focuses a basic problematic issue for Romantic literature: the relationship between beauty and passionate desire. In Romanticism beauty is associated with perfection and transcendence. Desire, passion, fantasy may necessarily lead the person to the beautiful but only to be jettisoned, like a starter rocket, once the *schöne Seele* soars free from the gravitational pull of desire, in the weightless purity of a transcendent realm. This is the autobiographical story of Wordsworth's "She Was a Phantom of Delight." Stendhal in the tradition of the literature of passion-love insists that beauty not lose its tie to its originating impulse, passion.

So if beauty dazzles like diamonds or crystals and thus distorts the "reality" of the beloved or of the relationship, it helps, in passion-love, to recover and underscore a deeper reality, that of the psychological fullness of the lover risking to abandon the unconscious security of solitude, the history of wandering lonely as a cloud.

Stendhal repeatedly correlated the possibility for passion-love with the prevailing political system or condition. It thrives amidst moderately liberal conditions, not so autocratic as to suppress all freedom for the individual but not so democratic (as in the United States) as to dull the desire for more individual freedom, for desire itself. Thus passion-love has its own politics; it implies resistance to or defiance of social conformity and suppression; it implies fulfillment of the individual past the limits to fulfillment officially or unofficially decreed by society. It follows that the literature of passion-love would embody the same contradiction as beauty, a contradiction between its definition as that which stands free from desire and the refusal to place it beyond desire.

Adolphe: The Contingencies
of Love

Love, the subject of so much Romantic literature, is the scene of ideological strife and a question: given the Romantic insistence, from Rousseau on, upon the originary nature of at least one kind of love, *amour de soi,* its purity and seminal strength, its basic goodness, why isn't the love between man and woman simply a synergism of two *amours de soi*? Paul and Virginia, two children of nature who love each other thus before puberty, are a powerful late-eighteenth-century test case of Romantic love. Bernardin de St. Pierre brings Virginia back to her lover after a prolonged immersion in the social life of Paris. Unpredictably, she returns still in love with Paul, but as her boat approaches the island of her youth, a storm—as violent as the most wonderfully violent lovemaking—sends her to her death. "True love" reveals merely the banality of sublime tragedy.

It is no accident that the popular *Paul et Virginie* was introduced and translated into English during the French Revolution by the radical Helen Maria Williams. The ideology of *amour de soi* fails the test of erotic love.

Romantic novels of passion-love situate themselves amidst contingencies. *Adolphe* is one of the harshest Romantic novels of the contingent nature of love. In *Adolphe* (completed 1810) this means that every gesture by the protagonist in the direction of his freedom, pleasure, and happiness ends in a tightening of the bonds of dependency and sadomasochism. Like Rousseau in the second half of his *Confessions*, Adolphe finds that his wish to proclaim his indifference to those around him, his wish to be alone, produces hostility from his acquaintances: they won't let him alone. When he finally tells Ellenore that he no longer loves her and she faints, he says: "I found myself more deeply committed than before."[1] His commitment does not feel to him like guilt; rather he feels the renewal of love. In this regard he painfully asks himself: "I have never acted out of cold calculation and . . . I have always been guided by true and natural feelings. How is it that, with these feelings, I have, for so long, merely caused my own unhappiness and that of others?"[2] Others' efforts to act on his behalf may cause similar uncalled-for results, as he says to his father: "Thinking you are separating me from her, you may well attach me to her forever."[3]

Rousseau, in his *Confessions*, asks us to judge him on his *intentions*, which are pure and kind and based on the sentiment of existence. The perversity or moral outrageousness of his actions may be condemned as such, but do not (he pleads with the reader) impugn his character (based on his intentions). The reader intervenes in the *Confessions* as a rescue fantasy. *Adolphe* is Rousseauist in this sense, but the separate realm of intentional innocence in this novel has very little power—only an echo of Rousseau. That Adolphe's actions continually undermine his intentions never leaves our consciousness; contingencies are simply too strong. The death of the heroine and the eventual wasteland wandering of the hero attest to the slow death of the sentiment of existence as the supreme fiction of Romanticism.

The ending of the novel brilliantly opens a dialogue—between the possessor of the manuscript and its eventual publisher—about the value and power of the story. The possessor sees it with enormous sympathy for its characters and their passion-love. Clearly an intelligent Romantic, he sees the lovers as producing and entangled in a system of emotions intolerable to the immediate society. He is moved by the psychological character of Adolphe's narrative. He has sympathy for the woman. Adolphe, he says, is a victim of his psychological makeup. In this interpreter, one senses the same consciousness that Stendhal and Hazlitt possess, and a political temperament willing to encourage the destablizing implications of passion-love, the fullness of human experience even if it is tortured and perverse.

The publisher also wants to publish the book, but for politically conservative and good economic reasons. The book would sell, he claims, because it is a morality play about excessive pride coupled with weakness of character. From his point of view the story exposes the failure of persons of erotic and passionate excess. When he says, "Circumstances are of little importance, character is everything," he denies that contingencies make up character or contribute in primary ways to actions. He is thus against psychology and fundamentally for the idyll of moral fortitude.

That Constant would end his novel with this exchange suggests that he understands the volatility of his subject, passion-love, in the psychosocial atmosphere of the early nineteenth century. He also understands the ambiguities of modern art: that the art object contains a volatile subject does not mean that it *acts* with volatility. But, then again, the reader—not as a rescuer—may *will* the volatile, destabilizing material out of its safer confines and allow it to resonate with the destabilizing social and psychological forces of which he is in the midst.

[46]

"She Was a Phantom
of Delight"

At first glance this poem celebrates the poet's wife. She has the magic to bewitch a man, she has domestic capacity both with the labor of the home and in the various expressions of domestic love, and she has "depth" or transcendent completeness. She reveals within herself the sentiment of existence. Better yet, these qualities seem to have evolved. She is to be praised for having *matured*. That the poem has obviously been written in the spirit of love is also to her credit: she is bathed in the love she has given.

Let me look at the poem "upon nearer view."

Suddenly the woman disappears, becomes again "a Phantom," and the poet appears instead—all eye:

> When first she gleamed upon my sight;
>
> . . . .
>
> I saw her upon nearer view,
>
> . . . .
>
> And now I see with eye serene. . . .

The poem is really the autobiography, the maturation of the poet's gaze, "the growth of a poet's m(eye)nd."

The opening stanza predicts a poem of passion, the destabilizing possibilities emanating from masculine fantasies: Werther meeting Lotte, St. Preux Julie, Hazlitt Sarah Walker, Keats (who compared himself to St. Preux) Fanny Brawne.

> A lovely apparition, sent
> To be a moment's ornament;
>
> . . . .
>
> A dancing Shape, an Image gay,
> To haunt, to startle, and way-lay.

This is the initial stage of Stendhal's crystallization, the phenomenon of the distortion of the lover, the normal psychosis, that leads to the epic complexities of modern adult psychosocial life. He knows a loss of control, drawn into the air of desire like the opening bud into the vulnerable flower.

Crystallization works only if the lover submits to the consciousness of the beloved's mobility, her independence. He must agree that she too knows the loss of control, and delight. The poet, in the next section of "Phantom," marks her freedom but severely limits it to the home: "Her household motions light and free, / And steps of virgin-liberty." No longer is crystallization possible. With the end of woman's delight, the woman becomes a shade, a phantom, a comfortable domestic anachronism, a trophy.

In the final section crystallization has vanished for the *Aufhebung* to the sentiment of existence. *Amour propre*—complex, social passion—yields to serenity. The eye rests forever open, in a gaze which has created a comfortable subjectivity. Desire for the woman has become contemplation of "Being," which is finally contemplation enamored of the beauty of the poet's own private history of maturation, the history of his gaze.

But what, really, of her delight? Where is it? Was it, like his, lurking in the margins (twilight and dawn) of the day? His claim that the gleam she cast has now become "angelic" light belongs to his story of himself.

> A perfect Woman, nobly planned,
> To warn, to comfort, and command;
> And yet a Spirit still, and bright
> With something of angelic light.

What has happened to Mary Wordsworth's delight?

47

Wordsworth's Late Poetry

about Women

The paradigm of the Romantic poem represents a test of the powers of selfhood to resist or transcend any invitation to erotic destabilization—whether the unhinging of the self would follow from a startling, haunting immersion in the erotic field or from the slower beguilements of erotic indolence or idleness. That the recently discovered love letters of the Wordsworths make perfectly clear an exuberant libidinal energy shared and delighted in proves that the poet's tendency to write about women in order to write about passion (only to triumphantly put it behind him) was a conscious (probably ideological) choice. Wordsworth's later poetry about or to women reveals basic elements of his understanding of the poet's function as he approached the Victorian era. Some of the late poems to women (e.g., Mary Wordsworth, Sara Hutchinson, and Isabella Fenwick) remind me of the seventeenth-century poem of meditation, a spiritual exercise, a maneuver to discover the spiritual in the fleshly, the permanent in the impermanent, to find through woman the intellectual facility and energy to make a stand against death. In woman he marks the permanent, inner light of love. Now, in one sense this should not surprise us; it is both natural and gracious for this Christian poet to write thus of his more or less elderly female companions. Yet in most instances, the praise of the "refined form" of a "soul-gifted Maid" is not casual, barely occasional, but rather contrived with the greatest urgency.

So much of the late Wordsworth seems, in a very literal sense, "defensive." All intellect and poetic craft are pitched toward erecting a bulwark, a structure against mortality, a watchtower from which all hints of dissolution can be anticipated and contravened, very like the little hill called "the Mount" on the lawn below the Lake District home at Rydal Mount from which ninth-century inhabitants could warn of approaching border raids from the north.

And just as Rydal Mount (where all these poems were written) is perfused in an atmosphere of various charm—the rugged mountain behind and above the house and the placid, shimmering lake below the trees—so these poems, once their archaic defensiveness is assumed, often open to a free space of geniality, of generosity and love.

My Rydal Mount analogy suggests the possibility that the old man Wordsworth struggled with his writing in an interesting way, that his associations about women and his associations about writing are related and are related through the trouble of eroticism.

If women are sources of his erotic fantasy and entanglement, so are the paintings in which they appear. Wordsworth stands in two guises before the painting of a woman: first, as observer of the woman and the painting, and second, as an artist at once identified by vocation with the painter and yet distinguished from the painter by his medium and possible intention.

The fate of the poet before the woman lies in his gaze. When Orpheus turns for an instant to catch the image of Eurydice, he loses her to endless night. For Wordsworth the instantaneous gaze is dangerous only if it is not prolonged past the moment of desire. The poet must look long and so must the lover who wants happiness, and so also must the beloved who wants, as he advises Mary, to be content with lost physical beauty: Don't, he says (in 1824),

> rate too high what must so quickly fade,
>   So soon be lost.
> Then shall love teach some virtuous Youth
> 'To draw, out of the object of his eyes,'
> The while on thee they gaze in simple truth,
> Hues more exalted, 'a refined Form,'
> That dreads not age, nor suffers from the worm,
>   And never dies.

And in a sonnet of the 1830s to Mary about her portrait painted by Margaret Gillies he begins with the history of his gaze:

> Though I beheld at first with blank surprise
> This Work, I now have gazed on it so long
> I see its truth with unreluctant eyes;
> O, my Beloved! I have done thee wrong,
> Conscious of blessedness, but, whence it sprung,
> Ever too heedless, as I now perceive. . . .

The erotic, subsumed immediately into the category of the mortal, seems to vanish, before the prolonged gaze, into the spiritual and eternal, the true or essential self that it is the painter's genius to record or more typically imply and the subject's virtue and good fortune to reveal.

But the poet realizes his proper vocation when he can simplify, purify the painting of its ambiguity in appearance and color, which is finally its ambiguity in erotic and spiritual intention. The painting stands before him representing the field of moral challenge. Does one yield to the power of color and image (which Wordsworth associates with desire and fantasy) or see through them with, as he says, "the inner eye"? The poet instructs the viewer of the painting how to exercise the eye beyond appearances. Thus, painting stands in need of poetry:

> Words have something told
> More than the pencil can, and verily
> More than is needed, but the precious Art
> Forgives their interference—Art divine,
> That both creates and fixes, in despite
> Of Death and Time, the marvels it hath wrought.

Who is the person capable of such visionary penetration? He is, according to the poem "Lines Suggested by a Portrait from the Pencil of F. Stone," a monk. Or, as he says in another painting poem, one who "drew a juster judgement from a calmer view," one who writes "with a spirit freed from discontent" and tries

> to recall the truth by some faint trace
> Of power ethereal and celestial grace,
> That in the living Creature find on earth a place.

Yet this longed-for disinterestedness which, more accurately, puts a lock on passion and erotic fantasy, becomes the goal of the poet's moral and psychological struggle.

In 1828, inspired by a painting by a contemporary, James Homes, Wordsworth wrote "The Gleaner," a lyrical apostrophe to the young, sensual woman in the painting, a poem that offers in two stanzas the momentous lure of her beauty only to retract or sublimate it in the final stanza. The painting, set across from the poem in *The Keepsake* for 1829, the anthology in which "The Gleaner" first appeared, captures the eighteenth-century iconography of sensual idleness, the fleshy "country girl" (as the poem was originally titled) sitting complacent in the warm, autumnal landscape and supporting across her lap a fine, thickly drooping sheaf of corn, or wheat.

How will the poet engage this vision of dangerous idleness? "The Gleaner" can be analyzed as a simple cultural program; it follows, lays bare what at the beginning of this section I proposed as a formula for many of the greater and lesser Romantic lyrics.

Idleness here occasions sensual and visionary fantasies, as it did for Werther, Adolphe, and other Romantic lovers, and as it did for Keats, words and phrases from whose odes occasionally in the late 1820s and the 1830s find a path through the heart of Wordsworth's lyrics. The opening section of "The Gleaner" acknowledges this cultural situation and, as he gazes upon the country girl, the poet's initial receptivity to it. "Fancy," says Wordsworth,

> sped
> To scenes Arcadian, whispering, through soft air,
> Of bliss that grows without a care. . . .

The second section of the poem acknowledges the danger to reason and sobriety:

> had thy charge been idle flowers,
> Fair damsel, o'er my captive mind,
> To truth and sober reason blind,
> 'Mid that soft air, those long-lost bowers,
> The sweet illusion might have hung for hours!

This sweet illusion hanging in soft air surely derives from the confusion of mind and sense in which Keats, in the "Ode to a Nightingale," immerses himself:

> I cannot see what flowers are at my feet,
>   Nor what soft incense hangs upon the boughs,
> But, in embalmed darkness, guess each sweet. . . .

Or, to recur to another beautiful instance of Wordsworth idle before the portrait of young Jemima Quillinan (1834):

> Beguiled into forgetfulness of care
> Due to the day's unfinished task; . . .
>   oftentimes and long
> I gaze upon a Portrait whose mild gleam
> Of beauty never ceases to enrich
> The common light. . . .

The poet as observer of female beauty and the poet as an artist identifying with but also interpreting another artist are saved, in the final stanza of "The Gleaner," from idleness, with its attendant dangerous fantasies, by the sheaf of corn. One must, it turns out, see past its languorous heaviness to its *use*. For corn, or wheat, becomes bread, and all who will eat it must

> Ponder the blessing they entreat
> From Heaven, and *feel* what they repeat,
> While they give utterance to the prayer
> That asks for daily bread.

Thus the country girl's sensuality is actually coincidental, as are the fantasies she stimulates in the gazer; more properly that wayward habit of mind, through the poet's careful and single-minded interpretation of the painting, needs to be revised into the exercise of prayer.

Wordsworth is aiming, it should be obvious, to represent the control of fantasy and idleness. Moreover, as an artist apparently vying with or correcting the painter's ambiguous lines and colors, the poet often redraws, quite literally, the portrait according to the rules of his monkish imagination. He would rather give this redrawn, deerotized portrait to his reader, preferring for the reader the chastening distance of the imagination to the excitability of the proximate gaze.

In contrast to these meditations on female portraits, the late poem "Lyre! though such power do in thy magic live" (published in 1842) begins (closer to Ovid than to his contemporary Tennyson or to the earlier Wordsworth of abandoned women) with a scenario like that of Apollo chasing Daphne, or Pan Syrinx. Exclaims Wordsworth of an unnamed Maid: "detain the lovely Fugitive."

> Lyre! though such power do in thy magic live
>   As might from India's farthest plain
> Recall the not unwilling Maid,
>   Assist me to detain
>   The lovely Fugitive:
> Check with thy notes the impulse which, betrayed
> By her sweet farewell looks, I longed to aid.
> Here let me gaze enrapt upon that eye,
> The impregnable and awe-inspiring fort
> Of contemplation, the calm port
> By reason fenced from winds that sigh

Among the restless sails of vanity.
But if no wish be hers that we should part,
A humbler bliss would satisfy my heart.
Where all things are so fair,
Enough by her dear side to breathe the air
Of this Elysian weather;
And on or in, or near, the brook, espy
Shade upon the sunshine lying
Faint and somewhat pensively;
And downward Image gaily vying
With its upright living tree
'Mid silver clouds, and openings of blue sky
As soft almost and deep as her cerulean eye.
Nor less the joy with many a glance
Cast up the Stream or down at her beseeching,
To mark its eddying foam-balls prettily distrest
By ever-changing shape and want of rest;
Or watch, with mutual teaching,
The current as it plays
In flashing leaps and stealthy creeps
Adown a rocky maze;
Or note (translucent summer's happiest chance!)
In the slope-channel floored with pebbles bright,
Stones of all hues, gem emulous of gem,
So vivid that they take from keenest sight
The liquid veil that seeks not to hide them.

The Dove Cottage manuscripts of this very dexterous and elusive poem help to bring to it more than just casual interest, for in one draft (among many laboriously done) the lovely Fugitive is named: Emma, Emmie, or Emmeline, of course, was Wordsworth's code name for his sister Dorothy in *Home at Grasmere* and several early lyrics. If Dorothy is meant, then the poem is pulled by a pathetic undercurrent; probably written in 1841, "Lyre!" would refer to the Dorothy struck by nervous and mental disorder, truly a fugitive from ordinary social intercourse and consciousness, hovering—even on sunny days—in her room before the fireplace. The letters tell us that the one stimulant to clear thinking and lucid and pleasurable communication was poetry—her own, Wordsworth's, or anyone else's. So Wordsworth calls upon his "Lyre" as the sure therapy to recall her to him, for he too must be lonely. Gazing enrapt upon that eye, once reputed "wild," he then drops down a key in intensity to beg the "humbler bliss" of viewing the Rydal torrent together; how often do the Grasmere Journals, the Recollections, and various poems record the deep trust of that mutual teaching?

Yet the playful spirit of the poem would seem to contradict the designation of Dorothy as the not unwilling Maid, unless the poet were caught in a wild nostalgia. Luckily, another Emma or Emmeline is at hand—Emmeline Fisher, teenage daughter of a cousin, a poet prodigy, whom Wordsworth first met in 1837 and who visited him at Rydal Mount in 1841. The poet was utterly infatuated with her and her poetic talents as was she with him. They too observed the Rydal torrent together; for them too poetry would be the preferred medium of pleasure. For a brief period during her visit to Rydal Mount, Emmeline went on a short trip with another relative: neither she nor Wordsworth liked the separation; could poetry call back *this* lovely Fugitive? As he often did with women he cared about, Wordsworth became proprietary: Emmie should not publish her exquisite poems too soon before the vicious literary public. Like a wood sprite in an Arcadian forest she as poet should remain untouched and undefined by the world. When Wordsworth died, she had not published any poems, but not long after his death her volume appeared and even went into a second edition.

With Emmeline Fisher as the not unwilling Maid, the poem's urgency or, as Dorothy Van Ghent says of Keats's Odes, its *emergent* intensity, makes more sense, as do the lines of animation between them:

> Check with thy notes the impulse which, betrayed
> By her sweet farewell looks, I longed to aid.
> Here let me gaze enrapt upon that eye. . . .

Yet true to form all the liveliness of passion gets quite beautifully redirected to the natural scene; both the poet and his Emma gaze together, as if at a painting, upon a wonderfully varied world of natural movements and colors. In a general way the poem has the same wishful construction as the last section of Keats's "Ode to Psyche," yet the fantasies and desires of love hinted at simply ripple harmlessly over the water and through the sunlight.

That "Lyre!" can make room for such extravagantly disparate female figures as an infirm, old woman evoking only sharp sadness and memories and a young, vital lady whose road lies all before her suggests that for Wordsworth passion and erotic desire, indices in the late eighteenth and early nineteenth centuries of male recognition of female otherness, are fugitive. One need only contrast this and the other poems considered here with the love poems of Byron, Keats, and Shelley to see the difference. Desire is fugitive, fleeing before the formal propriety of religious meditation. The potentially emergent power of a romantic poetry to and of woman finally flees acknowledgment of *her*. At her liveliest and happiest, she reverts to the chaste and childlike gaiety of the Thracian wood nymph: she

> Would gladly vanish from a Stranger's sight;
> Though where she is beloved and loves,
> Light as the wheeling butterfly she moves. . . .

48

Fanny Brawne: The

Woman's Delight

The gaze is a solution for Wordsworth. For Keats it becomes a problem
because the woman's delight is for him too palpable, and the gaze will not
register it fairly. The gaze claims to give the man too much power, power
that he knows he does not have and only ambivalently wants. His fantasies:
they are all about power and control; yet in the late lyrics to Fanny Brawne
he writes urgent wishes, prayers, ejaculations, hardly the syntax of power.
From the Odes on, sight—the sense of masculine power—fails him:

> Surely I dreamt today, or did I see
> 　　The winged Psyche with awakened eyes? . . .

> I cannot see what flowers are at my feet,

> .　　.　　.　　.　　.　　.　　.　　.

> But, in embalmed darkness, guess each sweet. . . .

> Fade softly from my eyes, and be once more
> 　　In mask-like figures on the dreamy urn. . . .

> Faded the sight of beauty from my eyes. . . .

> Bright star! would I were steadfast as thou art—
> 　　Not in lone splendor hung aloft the night
> And watching, with eternal lids apart,
> 　　Like nature's patient, sleepless Eremite,
> The moving waters. . . .

Or when sight does not apparently fail, it becomes imbued with touch,
taste, pain, memory—that is, it fails as an agent of power:

> 　　As when with ravished, aching, vassal eyes,
> 　　Lost in soft amaze,
> I gaze, I gaze!

> Who now, with greedy looks, eats up my feast?

What can I do to drive away
Remembrance from my eyes? for they have seen,
Aye, an hour ago, my brilliant queen!
Touch has a memory.

The distance of the gaze collapses in the presence of the desire it stimulates. The poet risks taste and touch, and the masculine fantasy of control is temporarily abandoned. He enters the circuit of a female desire and knows that it is there. He fears the loss of boundaries.

This is precisely where Keats's late poems arrive. They are not simply masculine fantasies of women as objects or witches. Marjorie Levinson has recently argued that eroticism in Keats is primarily masturbatory in character. Keats, she demonstrates, wrote a poetry self-conscious of the poet's (Keats's) alienation from that class—the aristocratic one—that would grant him access to the poetic tradition; and as a member of a middle class seeking identity through acquisition rather than inheritance, Keats chose to demonstrate this awkwardness subversively by presenting the machinery of acquisition more vividly than the acquisition itself. In the romance, for example, Keats would call attention less to the object of desire and its attainment and more to the self-absorption of the poet/hero in masturbatory fantasy. Support for this challenging and unsettling view comes not only from internal evidence but from those powerful early witnesses of his poetry, among others the reviewers of the 1817 volume of his poems, and from such figures as Wordsworth and most dramatically Byron, who found his work regressive, infantile, and frankly masturbatory. But while they may seem to participate in such fantasies, the late poems to Fanny Brawne possess a different urgency: there is, after all, a real Fanny Brawne, upon whose response to him Keats's sense of well-being rests. This poetry works in Stendhal's contemporary theory of "crystallization": the agonizing and contradictory passions of love lead the lover into love itself just as they heighten the resistances, widen the barriers, to love.

These poems project the masculine fantasy of a feminine focus of delight and conscious will. They are situated at the instant the poet, still surrounded by the expectations of (a constructed) masculine seeing, risks the sensation of (a constructed) feminine touch.

As the male poet yields to touch, he risks losing his masculinity in the bliss of touch. If, as Irigaray asserts, touch belongs fundamentally to feminine experience, what does it mean for the male poet Keats to write this way? Perhaps it means that he reaches out to describe an experience usually considered unavailable to the man, unsettling to the tradition of the masculine Romantic autobiographical lyric. And what is unsettling to the reader of the Romantic poem finally becomes too much for Keats:

> Let, let, the amorous burn—
> But, prithee, do not turn
> The current of your heart from me so soon.
> O! save, in charity,
> The quickest pulse for me.
>
> . . . .
>
> Give me those lips again!
> Enough! Enough! it is enough for me
> To dream of thee!

Romantic autobiography (e.g., Rousseau and emphatically Wordsworth) is the story of the gaze, the account of maturation away from touch and desire and fantasy. The distance created by the gaze does not collapse into the knowledge of the senses; the eye, instead, grows transcendently "serene." It is the story of masculine subjectivity, of the power over and effective annihilation of masculine fantasy and vulnerability. Indeed, for the Romantic autobiographer "the past," the period of immaturity, is the period of feminine sensation: "glad animal movements," or when "nature" haunted him like a passion. Sexuality was fluid.

Keats, in this regard, is no Romantic autobiographer. The poems threaten to burst their formal bounds; syntax is full of disruption. The mind works at a pitch of contradictory or scattered desires. Keats approaches the representation of the mobility of desire, which in turn approaches his knowledge of the multiple centers of feminine bliss. Both he and she are multiple, plural:

> all my fears,
> And hopes, and joys, and panting miseries.
>
> . . . .
>
> Voluptuous visions.
>
> . . . . .
>
> Whose heart goes fluttering for you everywhere.
>
> . . . .
>
> Love, love alone, has pains severe and many. . . .

The day is gone, and all its sweets are gone!
    Sweet voice, sweet lips, soft hand, and softer breast,
Warm breath, light whisper, tender semi-tone,
    Bright eyes, accomplished shape, and lang'rous waist!
Faded the flower and all its budded charms,
    Faded the sight of beauty from my eyes,
Faded the shape of beauty from my arms,
    Faded the voice, warmth, whiteness, paradise—

That shape, that fairness, that sweet minor zest
Of love, your kiss—those hands, those eyes divine,
    That warm, white, lucent, million-pleasured breast—

The writer of these poems (and of the letters to Fanny Brawne) was thought well into the twentieth century to have been diseased, crippled by bad reviews and incipient tuberculosis into writing distorted, eccentric, unbalanced, ugly verse. From a modern vantage point we have assumed this evaluation to be a function of Keats's highly passionate nature and his willingness to represent that passion in poetry. But along with passion, Keats's version of beauty may have upset Victorian and early modern readers. Wanting an image of "beauty without desire," they find instead a poet demanding that beauty and the desire for it appear in the same poem that collapses the traditional hierarchies of desire and its transcendence. Such poems may have more in common with Baudelaire than with Wordsworth, may be more urban than rural. Baudelaire's refusal, or inability, to write from an idyllic distance while at the same time longing for it takes poetry forever beyond the perspective of the early Romantics.

The "greater Romantic lyric" enacts the final suppression of masculine fantasies and of the knowledge of woman as subject at the same time it enacts masculine subjectivity autobiographically. Keats's Fanny Brawne lyrics depart significantly from this model, attempting to join to poetry a major subject of the politically progressive novelists, *l'amour passion*.

49

Passion and Lyric Form

in Epipsychidion

> Woe is me!
> The winged words on which my soul would pierce
> Into the height of love's rare Universe,
> Are chains of lead around its flight of fire.—
> I pant, I sink, I tremble, I expire!

The vision of love's rare Universe, elaborated in the lengthy passage preceding this one, appears to break off here in a catastrophe of the lover's self-consciousness. The fabric of intimacy, which the poet asserts on behalf of his imprisoned beloved Emilia, is thus different from that found in Coleridge's earlier "This Lime-Tree Bower My Prison," "Frost at Midnight," and Wordsworth's "Tintern Abbey." In those poems the desired vision of connection to and completeness with the beloved and with nature fills out the ending of the poem like wine filling up a goblet. Language and form satisfy and absorb the vision. Clearly Shelley intends the same result. So why doesn't it appear to work? I suggest that the new ingredient in Shelley is erotic passion, not its sublimation or transcendence (e.g., "She Was a Phantom of Delight") but its intensification and perpetuation. He wanted *Epipsychidion* published anonymously, and he insisted to Mary Shelley, his eventual editor as well as wife, that she not print it in his collected works. Shelley inherited from Wordsworth and Coleridge a poetic form for the expression of intimacy, but it was domestic intimacy—with wife or child or male friend. *Epipsychidion*, on the other hand, makes the representation of intimacy a problem by insisting upon the triangular, threatening and threatened, agony of erotic love: Percy, Emily, and her tyrannical father imprisoning her in a convent; Percy, Emily, and Mary. The autobiographical Romantic lyric enters the swift current of novels and dramas of erotic sensibility that challenge the stability and also the perceived tyrannies of domestic order.

So the poem seems a brilliant, necessary failure of the radical poetic temperament. Coleridge uses poetic language to escape into intimacy, that lime-tree bower, *his* prison; but Shelley's words, so enlivened with hope and desire, turn cruelly into the chains of solitary confinement, another Romantic disappointment. Like Wordsworth, defenseless as a wood where tigers roam, Shelley uses a literary language that at once terrorizes or stymies the poet and also occasions a great beauty, as the language intensifies and clearly produces a new world of language. Beauty often results when language withdraws from its instrumentality, its servitude to its referents. And, like Wordsworth in his Paris garret, Shelley is ambivalent about this new tumultuous beauty in language.

The ambivalence about beauty has its correlate in an ambivalence (cultural as well as Shelley's) about passionate love. Just as Werther's language of love leads to his annihilation, not simply by himself but by that domestic order he threatens but cannot destroy, so Shelley threatens to pierce love's rare universe but cannot break past the walls of Emily's convent and the walls of tyranny; his vision of love is annihilated. In this view Eros is power, linked to the struggle between domestic and adulterous love, between the family and the interloper. Erotic desire is supposed to win the struggle for the lover. But, just as usually happens in the novels, the lover loses.

If, however, Shelley's radical visionary impulse is taken seriously, the apparent disappointment rings with (as Roland Barthes says) the "catastrophe" of love's triumph. Shelley adopts a view of love opposite to that in the novels: instead of threatening domestic power and eventually being deflated or destroyed, the lover in *Epipsychidion* yearns for a love that flows out infinitely from the center. In one view love must be kept scarce; in the second love is abundant:

> True love in this differs from gold and clay,
> That to divide is not to take away.
> Love is like understanding, that grows bright,
> Gazing on many truths. . . . Narrow
> The heart that loves, the brain that contemplates,
> The life that wears, the spirit that creates
> One object, and one form, and builds thereby
> A sepulchre for its eternity.

This view flows into Shelley's vision of love on a paradisal island:

> Meanwhile
> We two will rise, and sit, and walk together,
>
> . . . .
>
> Possessing and Possest by all that is

> Within that calm circumference of bliss,
> And try each other, till to love and live
> Be one. . . .

Furthermore, a poem as intensely "poetic" as this, with its excessive piling up of metaphor, itself becomes a comedy of language. One might talk about the figurative extravagance in *Epipsychidion* as anxiety, and there would be plenty of instances in Shelley to support that. But one might also associate that extravagance with Shelley's visionary erotic temperament. In this second view the collapse of words near the end of the poem, part of love's "catastrophe," marks the visionary triumph of eros, as the pitch of desire, effluent and onrushing, fulfills itself at the expense of its vehicle, poetic language.

The tone of this poem, as Lionel Trilling once said about Keats's heroic deathbed remarks to his friends, is not ours. The phrase "winged words," in "The winged words on which my soul would pierce / Into the height of love's rare Universe," comes ultimately from Homer. I suggest that *Epipsychidion* is not cast in the mold of anxiety as much as it summons up a heroism, the heroism of love, such as one finds in the Cupid and Psyche story. When he opens the poem with

> My Song, I fear that thou wilt find but few
> Who fitly shall conceive thy reasoning,
> Of such hard matter dost thou entertain,

Shelley establishes an elitism that by the end of the poem rises to a heroic excess of energy seeking to pierce through the ordinary diffidence of the self in the face of its expansive possibilities. What is rare in love's universe is consciousness in love, mind erotically charged. The poet-hero, with the hero Psyche shining through the title of the poem, returns from his flight to disseminate his "weak Verses" (heroically his "winged words"), his vision among his friends:

> bid them love each other and be blest;
> And leave the troop which errs, and which reproves, —
> And come and be my guest, — for I am Love's.

The vision of conscious love scattered among his friends may refine Shelley's prayer to the West Wind to scatter the poet's words among mankind. The beauty of words functions not primarily to console (as at the end of Coleridge's "Dejection") but to enliven into consciousness and action.

Just as no warrior can stare into the brilliance of Achilles' divinely constructed shield and few mortals into the glowing figure of Psyche, how many of us can stare into the brilliance of Shelley's vision of love?

50

Dorothy Wordsworth's Scottish Recollections

For Mary Wollstonecraft beauty, produced in language primarily by the faculty of imagination, usually stands painfully at odds with social reality. "Imagination!" she exclaims in *Maria*, "who can paint thy power; or reflect the evanescent tints of hope fostered by thee?"[1] She would agree with Stendhal that beauty is "une promesse de bonheur," a promise of happiness, yet oppressive reality makes beauty seem like a dumb enchantment or charm, at best, as she says, "a refuge" or consolation. In the wonderful Scandinavian Letters,[2] analogous to Dorothy Wordsworth's Scottish *Recollections*, her words seem continually to fly away from any kind of descriptive engagement with present experience in order to make impassioned sociological observations and criticisms. Her language does not recover beauty in the service of happiness. So the passion and intensity cluster around indignant analyses of oppressive conditions and fervent formulations of improvement but—like Blake's Oothoon on the final plate of the *Visions of the Daughters of Albion*—hurtle into the void.

Virginia Woolf, comparing Wollstonecraft with Dorothy Wordsworth, sees precisely what happened to the passion and intensity as the latter tramped along a wet Scottish road:

> At last they reached the waterfall. And then all Dorothy's powers fell upon it. She searched out its character, she noted its resemblances, she defined its differences, with all the ardour of a discoverer, with all the exactness of a naturalist, with all the rapture of a lover. She possessed it at last—she had laid it up in her mind forever.[3]

All of Wollstonecraft's tragic ardor for social change channels into the comic ecstasy of Dorothy Wordsworth's descriptive and narrative records. The point is made continuously that Dorothy Wordsworth's writing lacks the self, the "I" that organizes so much of the masculine poetry of Romanticism. It is a point that, I think, excessively reduces the concept of self to a narrow caricature of self, a purely contemplative ego that dominates the outer world with a sense of the superiority of its inner life. In the *Recollec-*

tions Dorothy Wordsworth's self is everywhere present, almost breathlessly so; but it is the self in a kind of rapture with the scenes it *penetrates*. Woolf's observation, "all Dorothy's powers *fell upon* it," is metaphorically accurate; gravity is at work, the weight of her eagerness to describe and know her surroundings seems to overwhelm the power of conscious will to describe and know. Weight here is the passion and the ecstasy recorded in experience and producing her writing. The intensity, as Woolf says, gets laid up in her mind:

> Just as we began to climb the hill we saw three boys who came down the cleft of a brow on our left; one carried a fishing-rod, and the hats of all were braided with honeysuckles; they ran after one another as wanton as the wind. I cannot express what a character of *beauty* those few honeysuckles in the hats of the three boys gave to the place: what bower could they have come from? We walked up the hill, met two well-dressed travellers, the woman barefoot. Our little lads before they had gone far were joined by some half-dozen of their companions, all without shoes and stockings. They told us they lived at Wanlockhead, the village above, pointing to the top of the hill; they went to school and learned Latin (Virgil), and some of them Greek (Homer), but when Coleridge began to inquire further, off they ran, poor things! I suppose afraid of being examined.[4]

The scene immediately challenges her eye toward the beautiful and consequently toward that "promise of happiness." The passage I have quoted is visionary and Dorothy Wordsworth moves around in the vision. There is a wish to discover the beautiful in the here-and-now, but enfolded within that wish lies the silent acknowledgment of the inexpressibility of the beautiful, the future of happiness. Coleridge's comic intervention, making one think of Keats's censure of his "irritable reaching after fact and reason," scatters the possibility of beauty as the promise of happiness.

I think that she seeks to attach herself, through the power of her language, to the sources of life and to give back the corresponding energy. It is when one interprets her as victim, or as one fully defined by masculine principles, biases, and injustices in both her life and writing that that energy and feminine vision get missed. Put in a more sinister way, one suppresses the language of bliss, of passion, of the radiant inexpressibility of happiness. Here is another visionary passage:

The three fellow travelers—Dorothy and William Wordsworth and

Coleridge—arrive in the town of Lanerk, near which are famous waterfalls. Before they have even found an inn for the night, Wordsworth alone heads for the falls, leaving his sister and Coleridge adrift in a dirty if not uninteresting Scottish town. In his notebooks from the tour Coleridge rails and rages at Wordsworth for this kind of high-handedness and imperiousness. Surely the sister feels the same. Given this injustice, we as readers are poised at a crucial threshold. Do we let the poet's not so sublime ego dominate our response to Dorothy Wordsworth's rendering of the events that followed, seeing them as compensatory, rationalizing, submissive and resigned, even elegiac? Let us follow closely with our guide, now apparently bound in a dirty inn with the author of "This Lime-Tree Bower My Prison": "We were tired, however, and rejoiced in our tea." She continues:

> The evening sun was now sending a glorious light through the street, which ran from west to east; the houses were of a fire red, and the faces of the people as they walked westward were almost like a blacksmith when he is at work by night. I longed to be out, and met with Wm., that we might see the Falls before the day was gone.[5]

To label this passage "ambivalent" is to deny its power and also its nature. Rather Dorothy Wordsworth contacts multiple sites or sources that ignite her imagination and concentration. It's not a matter of deciding where she wants to be; she is not primarily working amidst an internal perception of scarcity. Indeed, her cathexis to the world exceeds its objects. The stunning vision of the lower-class people in this poor, unkempt town with its vivid, Blakean analogy to the laboring blacksmith, all made hellishly beautiful through having been steeped in the evening sun's rays, is (in the lingua franca of the Revolution) "glorious." We are not witnessing the ruralizing and distancing of the urban scene by means of the sun's light that consoles Wordsworth in "Westminster Bridge." At the same time, the sister's wish to join her brother at the waterfall couldn't be more urgent. I suspect that, at least in the moment of the writing, the provocation and stimulation of the first experience urged her into the yearning for the second. Indeed, the next part of the episode recounts her search for her brother and his simultaneous search for her.

She concludes the passage with a social comment based on her observation of the two guides, the little girl with her and a little boy with William:

> What a difference between the manner of living and education of boys and of girls among the lower classes of people in towns! she had

never seen the Falls of the Clyde, nor had ever been further than the porter's lodge; the boy, I daresay, knew every hiding-place in every accessible rock. . . . [6]

Perhaps this is a veiled or even unconscious comment about her own fate in this episode, but far more important and evident is its intentional effect and the personal context: shielded and animated by love, unlike the exposed Mary Wollstonecraft in the Scandinavian Letter, she reaches by means of her sympathetic and educated perceptions into the social fate of others.

In the episode just recounted one does not feel that the recovery from being left alone is compensatory, as in the comparable "This Lime-Tree Bower," in which the solitary poet turns fully to his solitude, to moralizing rationalization ("Nature ne'er deserts the wise and pure"), and to the rationalization—if one may call it that—of an image of beauty (the rook flying across the sun) that intends to bind together in imagination persons who are separated in fact. No, in this episode, rather, recovery is fulfillment, through testing and satisfying a range of human energies: a probing of the environment with senses and mind all alive.

The group of lyrics by Wordsworth included in the *Recollections* produces in the totality of the book a fine (and in Romantic literature unique) counterpoint of masculine and feminine dramas of self. Several of the best of these poems are constructed generally upon the "surmise," the play of mind in the act of probing or questioning the world, an act in which the poet is fundamentally less interested in discovery and in the world's response than in the mental play itself. "Glen Almain," "The Solitary Reaper," and "Yarrow Unvisited" all prefer to celebrate the abundance and idyll of inner visions and reveries. The world, like Yarrow, remains unvisited. In "The Solitary Reaper" the eye that is arrested becomes a speculum preserving the distance in ignorance while it converts and appropriates the content-full reaper's song into a wordless music to nourish the male poet's journey and self onward. As the masculine self grows firm in this interiorizing gesture, the edge of passion one feels in the act of probing and engaging the world softens. The radiant heat of possible encounter and transformation cools.

By contrast, *Recollections*, for all the placid exterior presumed in the eighteenth-century travel book, never suppresses that irradiating power, that restlessness, a restlessness which I think has to do with fulfillment and identity in the life of the woman. Dorothy Wordsworth, intently focusing on the women she encounters in the huts of Scotland, asks: "What sort of countenance and figure shall we see in this woman when we come into the light?" And the answer to such a question would not be singular since we are speaking of "This sex which is not one," the feminine consciousness the desires of which and pleasures and meanings do not focus, reduce, or cumulate into one. Dorothy Wordsworth, read through the mind of Luce Irigaray, would become a quintessential author of the feminine; her deep calm and her ecstasy, neither denying the other, played out through the language of nature, would appear sufficient and defining for the gender less taken with the need to interiorize, symbolize experience and more drawn to the multiplicity of surfaces; or—in the Jungian vision of the matriarchal consciousness—more drawn to the sources of life in the earth itself.

Yet, in Dorothy Wordsworth, to enter this realm of the feminine does not mean to sink into a kind of complacency with mere description (what one expects, perhaps, of that which Dorothy Wordsworth is not: a "maternal" consciousness). Recall, in the passage about the boys with honeysuckle sprigs braided in their hats, the sentence: "They told us they lived at Wanlockhead, the village above, *pointing to the top of the hill.*" This last gesture is the kind of "realistic detail" that analyses of narrative don't ordinarily deal with; it in this case could be said to contribute to the boredom of the reader hungry for narrative, symbolic structures. Such detail refuses to enter the symbolic realm, a realm that the reader can embrace as *meaningful.* Trilling speaks often of this kind of detail in traditional realistic narratives as the author's recognition of the "recalcitrance" of life in the face of the imagination's impulse to transform or incorporate life into itself and thus produce consolation. Barthes speaks of such fragmented, "interstitial notation" as the "direct collusion of a referent and a signifier," the "expulsion of the signified"[7] that comprises the very form of narrative itself. That meaning is resisted might constitute a particular otherness of the feminine. And when one considers Dorothy Wordsworth's traveling companions in Scotland, the two poets most responsible for erecting the edifice of the Romantic imagination, the faculty of internalization, unification, symbolicization; and when one adds that Dorothy Wordsworth was writing *Recollections* at the same time Wordsworth was writing not only the poems mentioned above but also major sections of *The Prelude,* the poem that *is* the edifice of imagination, then her recalcitrant details may be said to *intervene,* among other details absorbed by meaning, as the subversive contraries of feminine representation.

51

Childhood, or The Suppression
of Adolescence

1798 saw the appearance of another Gray in literature, along with Lamb's
Rosamund: Wordsworth's poem "Lucy Gray." Unlike Rosamund, Lucy is a
child untouched by erotic passion who dies a childhood death in the snow
only to be sublimed into a spirit of the place:

> —Yet some maintain that to this day
> She is a living child;
> That you may see sweet Lucy Gray
> Upon the lonesome wild.
>
> O'er rough and smooth she trips along,
> And never looks behind;
> And sings a solitary song
> That whistles in the wind.

The children portrayed by Wordsworth and Coleridge and much earlier
Rousseau and Goethe in *Die Leiden des jungen Werthers* belong to a pre-
Freudian world, without sexual and extravagantly possessive drives. They
seem to replace those adolescent or young adult figures of the decade of the
French Revolution—such as Blake's Orc or Oothoon, Godwin's Caleb Williams, or Wollstonecraft's Maria—whose unrestrained passions torment
the established and the powerful. In Goethe's novel the sight of Lotte and
her playful but obedient children puts the passion-ridden Werther into a
calm state, in touch with the sentiment of existence. The innocence of children in these works means a condition prior to the onset of passion, or a
condition cordoning off passion, the condition of the idyll.

But there were writers who seemed to interpret the pervasive representation of the passion-free child not as a psychophysiological fact but as a
cultural predisposition. Thus Blake sometimes juxtaposes, in his *Songs of
Innocence*, the language and culture of childhood with an illustration of adolescent female sexuality, as in his poems "The Little Girl Lost" and "The
Little Girl Found," as if behind the wandering innocence of the child Lyca
is the sexual drive to grow and explore. The shepherdess Thel, in *The Book*

of Thel, an adolescent quester, shrinks before the representation of her own sexuality back into the now empty idyll of her presexual childhood, and the illustration correspondingly interprets her retreat as an infantilization: an infant girl rides on the back of a thoroughly tamed loping serpent back to the vales of Har. Or, the reverse, the figure of Orc in *The Books of Urizen* as soon as he is born springs into adolescence and is pictured pressed body to body against the genitals and breasts of his mother Enitharmon. Or, the flower, in the poem "Infant Joy," associated with the idyllic childhood world, looks like flames, the image of adolescent erotic passion.

Rousseau, though longing for a vision of childhood evacuated of passion, seemed to know that passions existed in children. *Emile* is devoted to warnings about passion in very young people and the need to train and often divert it from its inclinations. Adolescence is the perilous time when the tutor must watch with extraordinary vigilance an incipient expression of sexual passion and rechannel it. Two generations later William Hazlitt and the young Romantic writers do not revise the notion of childhood so much as revise the early Romantic emphasis on childhood innocence as a locus of primary significance. Classic is Hazlitt's critique of Wordsworth's "Intimations Ode," in particular Wordsworth's doctrine of preexistence: "trailing clouds of glory do we come from God who is our home." He rejects this doctrine: "It is not from the knowledge of the past that the first impressions of things derive their gloss and splendour, but from our ignorance of the future, which fills the void to come with the warmth of our desires, with our gayest hopes, and brightest fancies. . . . In youth and boyhood, the world we live in is the world of desire. . . ."[1] Similarly, Shelley's *Alastor*, with its strong allusions to Wordsworth's Ode, can be read as a revision of the image of the innocent, presexual child into the adolescent questing for erotic love.

The later Romantics—Hazlitt, Keats, Byron, and Shelley—return, each in his own way, to the passion-love in the works of Rousseau, Goethe, and others, as if they perceived their parent generation of Wordsworth and Coleridge to have suppressed and displaced the main subject with idyllic childhood. The passion of the adolescent, as opposed to the chaste joy imputed to an idyllic childhood, may conjoin erotic desire and social consciousness, and may force recognition of the modern society's suppression of "the passionate other."

52

Burke, De Quincey, Stendhal

There is the thing; there is the thing made beautiful, covered or clothed in beauty. In Romanticism is there anything inherently beautiful? When responding to beauty, do we respond to the thing itself or to that drapery? The figure of Hermes may have appealed so much to Keats because the trickster god may have deluded us into thinking that what we saw as beautiful was, instead of the drapery, the thing. Ever since Plato beauty has stood in a hierarchical—either subservient or dominant—relationship to reality: is something beautiful more or less real than what we call real? And the related question is: what is that reality that the poet covers up with beauty?

Burke's image of drapery symbolized the manners and customs of civilization, the decency that provides stability, a kind of trust in the human community that without such drapery would revert to barbarity. He found that barbarity in the French radicals who, in their zeal for an abstraction called the rights of man, ripped the drapery off the royalty—the principle of continuity and trust—of France. The queen of France, by her imprisonment and eventual execution, was stripped of her noble and, what seems to be the same thing, her *chaste* beauty. It follows that the radicals cared nothing for beauty, and by their passion for principles brought about a fundamental ugliness that lies beneath civilization.

In this essay I have been searching for a beauty that appeals to the progressive elements in society, rather that reinforces and inspires those elements. The construction of such a beauty would, I have proposed, include reference to erotic passion and desire since, in Romanticism, they appear associated with the energy required to overcome the tyrannized consciousness, the mind-forged manacles. The liberation of consciousness often presupposes and includes the liberation of sexuality and the feminine subject.

Toward the end of the Romantic era two writers propose an image that shifts in the direction of sexuality the Burkean/Wordsworthian one of imagination as a covering of the real. Thomas De Quincey offers an image of beauty where parasitic flowers cover up a dead branch; Stendhal (in his theory of crystallization) says that when I fall in love, I see the glittering crystals that have formed upon a branch after it has been soaked in a super-saturated salt solution. The images have two things in common: (1) the "thing" is a branch or pole, that is, a phallic image, a sexual image, and (2) the allure is something that covers or hides the thing.

De Quincey, speaking of the structure and intention of his *Confessions of an English Opium Eater*, explains:

> the whole course of this narrative resembles, and was meant to re-semble, a *caduceus* wreathed about with meandering ornaments or the shaft of a tree's stem hung round and surmounted with some vagrant parasitical plant. The mere medical subject of the opium answers to the dry, withered pole, which shoots all the rings of the flowering plants and seems to do so by some dexterity of its own, whereas, in fact, the plant and its tendrils have curled round the sullen cylinder by mere luxuriance of *theirs*. Just as in Cheapside, if you look right and left, the streets so narrow that lead off at right angles, seem quarried and blasted out of some Babylonian brick kiln, bored, not raised artifi-cially by the builder's hand. But if you inquire of the worthy men who live in the neighborhood, you will find it unanimously deposed—that not the streets were quarried out of the bricks, but, on the contrary (most ridiculous as it seems), that the bricks have supervened upon the streets.
>
> The streets did not intrude upon the bricks, but those cursed bricks came to imprison the streets. So, also, the ugly pole—hop pole, vine pole, espalier, no matter what—is there only for support. Not the flowers are for the pole, but the pole is for the flowers. Upon the same analogy, view me as one (in the words of a true and most impassioned poet) *"viridantem floribus hastas"*—making verdant, and gay with the life of flowers, murderous spears and halberts—things that express death in their origin (being made from dead substances that once lived in forests) things that express ruin in their use. The true object in my *Opium Confessions* is not the naked physiological theme—on the con-trary, *that* is the ugly pole, the murderous spear, the halbert—but those wandering musical variations upon the theme, those parasitical thoughts, feelings, digressions, which climb up with bells and blos-soms round about the arid stock; ramble away from it at times with perhaps too rank a luxuriance; but at the same time, by the eternal

interest attached to the *subjects* of these digressions, no matter what the execution, spread a glory over incidents that for themselves would be—less than nothing.[1]

Beauty is associated with a phallic image, but not the way one would expect. Beauty emerges from masculine sexuality but does not belong to it. The relationship is parasitical; beauty, here associated with life, covers up, exists to hide and triumph over, the ugliness, the deadness, the *realness,* of the image of masculine potency. Clinically, the destructiveness of opium nonetheless produces, in a competitive way, the beauty of De Quincey's language and narrative.

It may be that beauty always stands at a remove from "naked" experience. At least it seems to in Romantic writing. One feels the sadness, the loneliness, in De Quincey's metaphors; the social and the psychological worlds are, however, more than simply inadequate for De Quincey: they seem to irritate him; he has no sympathy for or interest in them. He's more taken with his association of the streets of Cheapside to an ancient civilization than with their value and purpose for its present inhabitants. Indeed, while the passage insists upon the connection between social existence (in particular the social existence of the poor) and psychological existence and beauty, it treats those existences with loathing. With this seems to go a loathing of sexuality. And we are back with Edmund Burke.

With Stendhal's metaphor, beauty, illusion, psychological experience, and sexuality reinforce one another. The image of the beautiful salt crystals covering the branch, to be sure, is fragile. A stony-hearted reader might easily anticipate the dissolution of the dazzling image with one good rainstorm! But behind this fragility lies something sturdy and powerful, if very complex. Stendhal's *De l'amour*—written in a *Mischgedict* of treatise, anecdote, and aphorism—attests to the difficulty of explaining love but also to the immense importance of the subject. Sigmund Freud called this work one of the most significant studies of psychology in the nineteenth century, and Simone de Beauvoir called Stendhal a feminist.

For the glittering crystals, of course an illusion and a distortion, stimulate passion and fantasy, both of which are necessary for love. But paradoxically this dwelling in fantasy brings the lover closer to his or her psychological reality, that is, to a fullness of being. Late in the book Stendhal asserts that the best female lovers are those who have an independent life, who work. The male lover sees, and fantasizes, his beloved not as a static object but as a fluid, mobile independent subject. Crystallization stimulates a long, involved, risky process of producing, and improving upon, a human community. Beauty, glittering and evanescent, enhances the process of liberation.

53

The Romantic Essay: Cultural Criticism

and the Romantic Ego

Hazlitt and Lamb, through some of their essays, voice what with hindsight appears as a criticism of the poetic intent and method of the first generation of English Romantic lyric poets. Partly the criticism emerges in the chosen genre of the essay: at times they write as Romantic lyric poets estranged from poetry, turning to what De Quincey called impassioned prose. They accept the "enthusiasm" bequeathed by Romantic poetry (in fact transmitted through it from the eighteenth-century sentimental novel), what Blake calls "energy," and reject the wish to see and discover poetic imagery and language from a "disinterested," sublimated, spiritual position; Hazlitt, in particular, finds such inspiration a form of consolation. Similarly he questions the place of poetic beauty in its relation to knowledge and power, and accepts beauty only as it furthers consciousness. At their best *Lamb and Hazlitt expose the grandiosity of the Romantic ego,* its inclination to subdue the world and history and the waywardness of unconscious life to itself; and implicitly by the force of their writing they charge poetry with an elitism that renders it inadequate to the needs and the very fact of the rapidly expanding and broadly based readership in the 1820s. A survey of the nineteenth-century familiar essay after Hazlitt and Lamb quickly reveals that later essayists—to the extent that Hazlitt and Lamb are models—adhere to the consoling side of the Romantics' ambivalence; thus, I believe, the impulse in Hazlitt and Lamb to liberate sexuality, appetite, class consciousness, and the personal unconscious from the disarming, consoling imagination has been undervalued.

Several of Lamb's best essays appear to be about the fate of passion and sensuousness: are they to be released or, in the predictable design of the poets, to be subdued and disarmed?

In Lamb the major image of what constitutes domestication and imagination is the re-erection or repopulation of an old building; this, of course, is what happens in several of his most famous essays (e.g., "Blakesmoor in H . . . shire," "Christ's Hospital Five-and Thirty Years Ago," "The South-Sea House," "The Old Benchers of the Inner Temple," "Dream-Children:

A Reverie"). The principle of thought in such essays is—just as Virginia Woolf would have it—reverie, waking dream, association; and the effect at once envelops the reader and transcendentalizes him out of his present discomforts. The delight one often receives from reading this side of Lamb rests precisely with the sense of easy intimacy and the summoning of a mood of innocent regression. His memory of "Blakesmoor" could stand for this particular experience of the essay itself:

> Variegated views, extensive prospects—and those at no great distance from the house—I was told of such—what were they to me, being out of the boundaries of my Eden?—So far from a wish to roam, I would have drawn, methought, still closer the fences of my chosen prison; and have been hemmed in by a yet securer cincture of those excluding garden walls.[1]

There is more, however, to Lamb than this; many Victorian essayists would be content with writing themselves into a secure idyll of prose. But on the walls of one room at "Blakesmoor" (the mansion where years ago Lamb's grandmother had lived and which the most recent owner "had lately pulled . . . down") were Ovidian scenes of Actaeon and Marsyas. That is, in this tranquil, regressive recollection he discovers on the walls scenes of dismemberment and flaying—"Actaeon in mid sprout, with the unappeasable prudery of Diana; and the still more provoking, and almost culinary coolness of Dan Phoebus, eel-fashion, deliberating divesting of Marsyas."[2] This will serve our purpose as an image for his usual mode: the violence becomes decoration, is removed from the center of the room, where the family is, to the protective walls.

However, Lamb's essays take on unique life when he begins to take the violence off the walls, to explore the meaning of violence and sensuality. It looks like an inversion of his usual approach; for example, in "A Dissertation upon Roast Pig" it is surely significant that the discovery of roast pig occurs when buildings are *destroyed* (burnt to the ground) rather than *erected*. Indeed, says Lamb, the mania in "ancient China" for eating roast pig and the belief that roasting could be accomplished only by burning down the house that contained it caused people to build "slighter and slighter every day, until it was feared that the very science of architecture would in no time be lost to the world."[3] He seems to be moving far from that transcendentalizing aspect of imagination which, for example, Goethe praises (in *Von deutschen Baukunst*) as operative in the great Gothic cathedral at

Strasbourg: "How the vast building rose lightly into the air from its firm foundations; how everything was fretted, and yet fashioned for eternity."[4]

What emerges, for Lamb, from this tearing down of imagination?—The possibility of an essay that brings into striking convergence images of barbarity and the conditions of civility. The barbarous runs a spectrum from the killing of pigs to the intensity of the pleasure in excessive refinements of both eating and writing: the *relishing* of food and words. At this juncture of barbarity with civility there is much humor; but it is also disquieting, even repulsive that there should be such pleasure in the delicate roasting and tasting and then devouring of (he continually emphasizes) innocent, infant pigs . . . infant pigs. This, however, is no contradiction since humor itself signals a relatively undefensive posture towards reality, even in its most disturbing aspects. Lamb, in this regard, reveals a rigidity in the consoling imagination, a need to screen or subdue carefully all threatening material, just as a patriarch or monarch may need to weaken apparently subversive elements.

In "The Convalescent"[5] Lamb playfully dramatizes the transformation of such a monarchical or grandiose imagination into the humbler, object-related imagination of an essayist with deadlines to meet. Lamb and Hazlitt seem to charge the poets with excessive narcissism accompanied by a studied distancing of themselves from the historical world. In this essay the grandiosity, pleasurable as it may be, that accompanies the bedridden patient must give way to what is at once a diminished self-representation and an enlarged, more acute sense of his familiar world before anything but self-serving writing will take place. The essayist-as-essayist is no longer "monarch" of the sickbed with its "wavy, many-furrowed, oceanic surface," but must become sensible to "the magazines and monarchies of the world alike; to its laws, and to its literature." Here Lamb takes the question of narcissism a step further, for it appears that disease, even or maybe particularly a disease that gratifies the self, will biologically not permit writing: true genius is healthy, sane. And yet the wonder of this essay lies in the way it gives the impression of a convalescence itself: the movement from sickness to health, from self-absorption to other-relatedness. As the essay progresses, narcissistic pleasure withdraws from the center to the periphery of experience; yet, since the focus of most of the essay is the pleasures of illness, one cannot say that narcissistic pleasure has withdrawn at all. What definitely increases, however, is the foregrounding in the reader's mind of the obscure but undeniably crucial consequence of such pleasure in Romantic art. As in the "Dissertation upon Roast Pig," the pleasure described intimates its own potential dangers—here not only death itself but the severing of all social interest, of "interestedness"; and if the opposite here of interestedness is disinterestedness, then the latter approaches not the sublime or the condition of aesthetic negative capability but sheer oblivion. The writer of modern literature must keep the social, interested sense alive; this is the point of Lamb's alliterative parallelisms: magazines and monarchies, laws and literature.

54

Hazlitt's "The Fight"

"Mr. Shelley's style," said Hazlitt in 1824, "is to poetry what astrology is to natural science—a passionate dream, a straining after impossibilities, a record of fond conjectures, a confused embodying of vague abstraction— a fever of the soul. . . ." Hazlitt admired Shelley's intensity, his "single thoughts of great depth and force," his "single images of rare beauty."[1] But he criticized the poet for his grand conceptions which seemed to lose all touch with the recalcitrant materials of life, as if there were an undesirable elitism in Shelley's immaterialism.

About Wordsworth, for whom Hazlitt nonetheless has enormous respect as a poet of beauty, he says:

> No storm, no shipwreck startles us by its horrors: but the rainbow lifts
> its head in the cloud, and the breeze sighs through the withered fern.
> No sad vicissitude of fate, no overwhelming catastrophe in nature
> deforms his page. . . .[2]

Wordsworth is "reserved, yet haughty, having no unruly or violent passions, (or those passions having been early suppressed). . . ." Both of these poets of the beautiful are deficient in some important way, abstracted, attenuated in their relationship to the full range of human experience. Beauty itself, in other words, becomes a problem in relation to erotic passion and to social and class differences, a problem that Hazlitt, I believe, is constantly attending to in his essays.

Hazlitt, at the time of his remarks on Shelley, had just published his own novel of passion, *Liber Amoris*, which demonstrated his submission to erotic fantasy, just as did Keats's contemporary poems and letters to Fanny Brawne and Stendhal's *De l'amour*. All of these contribute to the revival of the representation of passion in the younger generation of Romantics. Hazlitt's novel is particularly interesting in that Sarah Walker, the object of his passion, comes from a lower class than he, a fact which he does not shirk in his novel. However, the piece that most provocatively and brilliantly engages new implications for the representation of passion is hardly (or not obviously) about erotic love at all, his journalistic essay on a boxing match, "The Fight," published in the *New Monthly Magazine* in 1822.

"The Fight" is one of the most passionately written pieces of prose in the later Romantic period, and it is about a passion, the passion for sport. Most of the essay takes place not at the scene of the fight between Bill Neate and Tom Hickman (known as the Gas-Man), but on the road to and from the fight and at various alehouses and inns along the way. No matter what people are talking about, the conversation is invariably pitched toward the fight and those who engage the culture of boxing, who are called the Fancy. The description of the fight is pumped up with enormous energy; the pages fairly explode with vivid writing about the characters of the fighters—the modesty of one, the arrogance of the other—about the punishment dealt out in seventeen rounds of bare-fisted blows, about the tough concentration and doggedness of the two men who, exhausted and battered, continue to eye each other with an aggressive caution and go for the knockout. "It was," says Hazlitt, "a good standup fight."

Hazlitt writes about a large, amorphous community, ranging from the lower-class fighters themselves to writers like himself. The essay is filled with talk, exchange of views, the making of arrangements, the parading— as with sports fans everywhere—of facts and statistics and reminiscences of great athletic feats. Passions fill the huge crowd as they rock to the blows of the fighters. Hazlitt's essay, quite clearly, extends the talk, the exchange, the passion about the fight into more talk for the readers of the *New Monthly Magazine*, talk that not only entertains but, as Werther said, "catches fire" in the imagination of that growing and amorphous reading public.

What, in Hazlitt's essay, might catch fire? The sparks fly with the clash of cultures and social classes. Hazlitt constantly intercalates his journalistic prose with slang from the Fancy, the fight crowd, and with quotes from high culture, from the canon (usually Shakespeare). Sometimes he will graft one culture onto the other, as in his epigraph, paraphrased from *Hamlet*: "The *fight*, the *fight's* the thing, / Wherein I'll catch the conscience of the king." This is a particularly pointed hybrid, given the perceived danger, to established order, of large crowds. Or, in his "involuntary fit of enthusiasm" of anticipation of the fight, he quotes from Spenser: "What more felicity can fall to creature, / Than to enjoy delight with liberty?" and says, "this, translated into the vulgate, meant *Going to see a fight.*"

In such "fits" the clash between popular and high culture, "vulgar" and refined sentiment, seems to occur. The climax of these clashes is reached with the main knockdown blow, where the shock of physical contact, the inversion of the human form by blood, resonates from the lower-class boxers to the reference to Dante:

Neate just then made a tremendous lunge at him, and hit him full in the face. It was doubtful whether he would fall backwards or forwards; he hung suspended for a second or two, and then fell back, throwing his hands in the air, and with his face lifted up to the sky. I never saw any thing more terrific than his aspect just before he fell. All traces of life, of natural expression, were gone from him. His face was like a human skull, a death's head, spouting blood. The eyes were filled with blood, the nose streamed with blood, the mouth gaped blood. He was not like an actual man, but like a preternatural, spectral appearance, or like one of the figures in Dante's *Inferno*.[3]

In the context of "The Fight" I will risk calling this passage "beautiful." Clearly for fight fans the passage is not "ugly," that is, inappropriate or subversive, although for high culture it might be. Nor ought we to call it "sublime," so terrifying that it demands that strenuous effort of mind and "reason" to recall oneself to a sense of superiority and disinterested and transcendent calm. One is not supposed to be recalled at all: the fight, the fight's the thing. The high density of metaphor, the allusions to myth and tradition give the account, as Hazlitt would say, a refinement. Hazlitt delighted in the fact that his fight companion P. G. Patmore brought with him to the fight a copy of Rousseau's *New Eloise* and exuberantly challenged: "Ladies, after this, will you contend that a love for the FANCY is incompatible with the cultivation of sentiment?" He said: "It's the highest thing I remember—a piece of real intellectual refinement. . . ."[4] The point is not that Rousseau cancels out or defeats the fight, but that the clash of the two cultures is pleasurable and liberating. In the same sense the description of the knockdown blow is beautiful.

But more needs to be said about the context of this moment of beauty, in terms of erotic passion. This is obviously a "man's" essay. All the main characters are men; they are brought together—in the ring, in the inn, on the stagecoach—because they are men. The readers, we assume, those who "will relish [his] account of" the fight, are men. Or are they? The jaunty sentence to ladies just quoted is matched by a taunting, bitter, mean-spirited passage in the opening paragraph:

Ladies—it is to you I dedicate this description; nor let it seem out of character for the fair to notice the exploits of the brave. Courage and modesty are the old English virtues; and may they never look cold and askance on one another! Think, ye fairest of the fair, loveliest of the lovely kind, ye practisers of soft enchantment, how many more ye kill with poisoned baits than ever fell in the ring; and listen with subdued air and without shuddering, to a tale tragic only in appearance, and sacred to the FANCY!⁵

Hazlitt's morbidity about women refers to the Sarah Walker affair which was causing him terrible heartbreak. (Indeed, in a passage canceled because of its extreme morbidity, one realizes how much a preoccupation with Sarah Walker underlies "The Fight.") *Liber Amoris* records his absorption in the sufferings of love with a woman who was ultimately indifferent to him. "The Fight" is the antiphonal voice where—in a forced effort to break from his misery in love—pleasure, passion, involuntary fits all occur in a world of men. Eve Kosofsky Sedgwick and René Girard have underscored, in her phrase, the "homosocial desire," in heterosexual relationships, the triangle brought about when the man's enticement to the woman is mediated by another man to whom the male lover may have unannounced attachments. Interestingly, *Liber Amoris* consists largely of letters to his male friend Patmore; and one recalls Werther driven wild by the peasant lad telling him about his love for an older woman, or wanting to kiss the messenger boy coming from Lotte, and finally the kisses given by the judge's sons to the lips of the dead Werther.

In the canceled passage Hazlitt remembers a time before women, a time of pure happiness: "I thought of the time when I was a little happy [thoughtless] [careless] child, of my father's house, of my early lessons, of my brother's picture of me when a boy, of all that had since happened & of the waste of years to come—I stopped, faultered, & was going to turn back once more to make a longer truce with wretchedness & patch up a hollow league with love—when suddenly the clattering of a Brentford-stage reminded me where I was."⁶ It looks as though Hazlitt's homosocial fantasy and the essay that follows occur at the expense of women, but it is not quite that simple. He wants to patch up the relationship, when the stage comes to take him to the fight and diverts him from his problems. But the sentence to the ladies about the compatibility of the fight with sentiment leads one to believe that the exuberance of the homosocial pleasures does not exclude pleasure with women, and that in fact some of the pleasure for Hazlitt derives from his representation of a truly heterogeneous, amorphous population and of an event showing the compatability of different cultures. The King of Hazlitt's epigraph would not have approved this gathering of happy men from different classes; nor presumably, would have taken to a work of art that celebrated it. Hazlitt might have used for his epigraph Blake's proverb of hell, "Exuberance is Beauty."

In many of Hazlitt's best essays, one encounters a persistent query: how should I assess the aesthetic values of the best poets of the day, Coleridge and Wordsworth, in light of their retrograde politics? Hazlitt usually identifies their commitment to the chaste aesthetic virtue of disinterestedness with conservative politics and, therefore, the disarming of erotic passion. The Coleridgean faculty of disinterestedness is, of course, the imagination. Hazlitt, though himself drawn to the imagination as a synthesizing and transcendental faculty, nonetheless seems to prefer the other aesthetic faculty—in Coleridge's hierarchy the lesser one—the Fancy, which for him is that which is more in touch with psychological, physical, and political reality. "How matter presses on me!" he happily exclaims, "What stubborn things are facts!" In "The Fight" he lightly but persistently puns on the Fancy, at once an aesthetic faculty and the culture engaged in boxing: "The FANCY are not men of imagination." Thus the clash between cultures deepens to include the problem of artistic representation. But the Fancy, that is, the faculty, also seems to attend to passion; indeed, poetry, he says elsewhere, ought to be the expression of the passions, which modern poets—to their detriment—want to suppress.

In "On Going a Journey" (1821) he quietly and somewhat ruefully argues against disinterestedness and "perspective": the ability to take in multiple moments, multiple points of view at one time. Coleridge, he says, could walk and talk at the same time: "He could go on in the most delightful explanatory way over hill and dale, a summer's day, and convert a landscape into a didactic poem or a Pindaric ode." Hazlitt's thinking-is-walking metaphor serves his conviction that we "comprehend the texture of our own being only piece-meal. In this way, however, we remember an infinity of things and places." To slightly shift the context, he means that the most important faculty is that which notes not similarity but variety and difference. The mind energized by desire, and not the serene soul, is the democratic faculty.

But what of the violence of the fight? the fact that the pleasures all derive from a "tremendous blow" that "made a red ruin of that side of his face"? First of all, it is the price of courage, and Hazlitt rails at the detractors of boxing: "Ye who despise the FANCY, do something to shew as much *pluck,* or as much self-possession as this, before you assume a superiority which you have never given a single proof of by any one action in the whole course of your lives!" But in the setting of this essay and in the context of others, the violence also reverberates as a vision of a nuclear explosion of classes: what kind of energy would it take for the literary culture and the culture of the Fancy to fuse? what would happen then?

[55]
Haidee's Father

In a typical eighteenth-century sentimental or Gothic novel or drama (e.g., *Clarissa*, *Julie*, *Emilia Galotti*, *Werther*, *The Italian*) a paternal figure usually opposes the passionate love between the protagonists. He drives the wedge into their joy and hope as a spokesman for the social and domestic status quo. Although he or she may find him a sympathetic figure, the reader also associates him with the dull, imperturbable, and finally securely powerful weight of the bourgeois domestic and sometimes imperialistic order. Even in Keats's late version, *The Eve of St. Agnes*, the world of dull paternal propriety hovers blindly but menacingly over the lovers in their dreamy ecstasy and descends coldly and firmly over the castle when they have left for Porphyro's "southern home." In Keats's *Lamia* the cold philosopher Apollonius stands in for society's patriarchal disapproval. All of these figures represent opposition to the full flowering of the individual and the full satisfaction and apotheosis of erotic love.

How unexpected (and how funny) does Byron's portrait of Lambro, Haidee's father, seem embedded in this tradition! Lambro is no dull figure, nor is he an upright pillar but rather a "piratical papa," who bears relation to the ruling class not through a penchant for control and oppression but through his illegal ways of making money. The difference is he practices without deceit:

> Let not his mode of raising cash seem strange,
>   Although he fleeced the flags of every nation,
> For into a prime minister but change
>   His title, and 'tis nothing but taxation;
> But he, more modest, took an humbler range
>   Of life, and in an honester vocation
> Pursued o'er the high seas his watery journey,
>   And merely practised as a sea-attorney.
>
> (*Don Juan*, III, 105–12)

Lambro lives not by suppressing his or anyone else's passions but by immersing himself in passion and sensuality. He is a patriarch who is also an outsider. Returning from piratical adventures to find that Juan and Haidee have not only become lovers but taken over his home and turned it into a perpetual orgy, he explodes in fury and with help from his men carves up Juan and drags him away from Haidee. But his paternal rage occurs with no resonance to opposed social orders or principles. At stake is not "domesticity" as the foundation of modern society. Nor is the expression of desire as a moral principle (as in Blake) at stake. It is simply a question of two opposing desires, of appetites; desire itself continues to pervade the world of *Don Juan*.

With his aristocratic complacency Byron does not explore the relationship between desire, or sexuality, and class. He will not observe the effect of imposed poverty upon sexual pleasure, as does Keats in his letter to his brother Tom when he writes from Scotland about the effect of the church on the poor: "These kirkmen have done Scotland harm—they have banished puns and laughing and kissing. . . ."[1] But in *Don Juan* desire is still the hero; it is kept free (and puns are not banished).

If we inquire about the fate of beauty in this poet contemptuous of the system of the opposing orders (unlike his liberal enemies Coleridge and Wordsworth), we cannot expect to find it in some transcendence of the "bad present." Instead we discover, embedded in the Haidee episode (with Lambro lurking around the edges of his daughter's orgy), the wonderful song of the local bard, "The Isles of Greece," which celebrates the beauty and glory of Greece in its poets as something to be recovered and renewed in the fight for its liberation:

> The isles of Greece, the isles of Greece!
>   Where burning Sappho loved and sung,
> Where grew the arts of war and peace,—
>   Where Delos rose, and Phoebus sprung!
> Eternal summer gilds them yet,
> But all, except their sun, is set.
>
>   I dream'd that Greece might still be free,
> For standing on the Persian's grave,
> I could not deem myself a slave.

This song of liberation hardly has the tone of ascetic sacrifice of the radical literature of the 1790s. Rather it mingles the spirit of sensual fatalism of the Greek Anthology with the beautiful proportions of dedication to the poetic tradition—its precarious vitality and the poet's civic calling to

preserve it—that one finds in Horace's Ode, IV, 9 ("ne forte credas inter-
itura quae"). Here the poet, asserting the need to preserve the image of the
consul Lollius, compares himself unfavorably with the poets of the Greek
tradition preserving the image of their heroes, just as Byron does: "And
must thy lyre, so long divine, / Degenerate into hands like mine?" But the
poet's calling remains firm even in the prosaic present. In Byron, unlike
the heroic poets of sensibility praised by Wordsworth and Keats (Chatter-
ton and Burns), the sacrifice comes not from excess of poetic spirit but
from a refusal to live under tyranny, a sacrifice not ascetic but preserving an
anacreontic independence: "Fill high the bowl with Samian wine!"

Just as Byron displays an irreverence for the symbol of the dull, tyrannical father figure, so he does not seem obsessed with the fate of the self
(as is typical of the English Romantic lyric). Byron shared with Keats and
the essayists an irritation with the egocentrism and (at times) grandiosity
often found in the early Romantics. To the degree that beauty is associated
with the assertion of the individual ego, Byron turns away. But if beauty is
defined in terms of exuberance and the effluence of passion, as in this lyric,
then Byron stands at the center of the tradition.

[56]

"A Stream Scarce Heard"

. . . all forms must tend toward abstraction, which, as we know, is not at all contrary to sensuality.

—Roland Barthes

In considering the contexts and strategies by which Wordsworth curtails, in his poems, the volubility of passion and sensuous experience, one can lose touch with his subtle knowledge of the passionate and the sensuous and the full precision of their evocation. How often do I experience, in reading, the "rustle of language" (Roland Barthes)! How often does language, incompletely understood as a message, nonetheless stimulate my thinking, excite or comfort me! This level of sexual apprehension, this eroticism of language, is something Wordsworth (and to a lesser degree other Romantic poets) knows and exploits. His poetry could have gone this way far more than it did, but in order to know Wordsworth more completely we must garner these moments. The surmise, discussed elsewhere in this essay as an elaborate fending off of knowledge, a kind of asceticism with regard to the world, nonetheless builds within its playful interiorizing of questions and alternatives the excitement of erotic purposiveness. Something similar happens in these lines from *Resolution and Independence*:

> The old Man still stood talking by my side;
> But now his voice to me was like a stream
> Scarce heard; nor word from word could I divide;
> And the whole body of the Man did seem
> Like one whom I had met with in a dream. . . .

So much of masculine Romantic poetics relies on the making of meaning, on the synthesis and control of materials. In that frame of mind we are tempted to see these lines as a form of Wordsworthian mysticism, a radical abstractedness from ordinary experience. But we can also see here the precarious availability to Wordsworth of the unacknowledged other of this poem, the feminine; the young poet yields momentarily, almost lazily, to the exciting comfort of meaningless sound, close to the aqueous source of life, close to the rooms of the mind in the unconscious largeness of dream.

I think that in our ordinary experience of this poem we incorporate this moment of vulnerability into the poem's intended architecture of resolution and independence of character. Indeed, since the fullest realization of self absolutely demands the conscious, if temporary, abandonment of control, we accept this moment as part of this poem naturally, gratefully. But it is important for me to acknowledge Wordsworth's acknowledgment of such a moment in this meditation upon a literary phenomenon, Romantic poetry, a poetry that often seems compelled to open such occasions of erotic vulnerability only to close them off. It is because of Romanticism's powerful intuitive apprehensions of the feminine, its acute perceptions of what constitutes the subversive in a society acutely alive to the subversive and harsh with it, that I have sought to mark some instances of the flickering, the trembling, of the other.

Return: The Sentiment
of Otherness

I began this essay with Rousseau's sentiment of existence and have arrived at the sentiment of otherness. How far have I really traveled? Rousseau fiercely described a condition of pure existence and the feeling emanating from it. Behind that fierceness lay his conviction that modern society does not like to leave the solitary person alone, that solitude—or independence—must be won not silently but aggressively, in his case even noisily. Part of the pathetic yet brilliant comedy of Rousseau emerges in his provocation of the other in the service of escaping it. Is the sentiment of existence, therefore, a fantasy of a formula for the return to the sources of life, or does it more authentically describe a modern Western effort to recover the archetype of the *nostos,* the return—after the journey through experience—home, the place of origins, remembered or unremembered, at once recovered and discovered? Rousseauian Romanticism, with its belief in the social evil and the corresponding affective entanglement, *amour propre,* still, I think, adheres to this archetype, but I do not think that Rousseau has constructed the most interesting, or hopeful, version of it.

The perception of the dominant writers in France and England during and after the period of the French Revolution was that government and its sympathizers are repressive, not only of actions but of sentiments; sentiment, passion, and desire mean an independence of spirit and mind directed toward an individual and communal happiness that appears threatening to established social structures. What is progressive in Rousseau is his recognition of this and his affirmation of sentiment, privacy, and intimacy—of *amour*. But what seems retrograde is his separation of the narcissitic passion (*amour de soi*) from the social one (*amour propre*). Other writers— such as Blake, Keats, and Hazlitt—do not make this distinction, or (in the case of Wordsworth) at least fight against it. Filtered through their work, Rousseau can appear cautious and severe with *all* desire. How paradoxical, given Rousseau's passionate prose and focus on the drama of feeling, that he could be accused of cutting off temptation at the root! But one can argue that the Romantic writers attempted to represent the liberation and the rationalization of social and erotic desires latent and conflicted in Rousseau. The affect of that representation I will call the sentiment of otherness.

Dorothy Van Ghent says of Keats's "Ode on Melancholy" (and of the Odes in general) that we are involved in "a true emergency, for something is to 'emerge' from it, a transformation of our sense of the world."[1] Enthralled by his own implicatedness in the loss of life and pleasure, Keats in his shorter poems is *urgent* in the presence of death. The Odes, written in the aftermath of his brother Tom's death, enact the gloom or fatality of eros ("At a touch sweet Pleasure melteth") under the sign of hope. Beyond ordinary consciousness lies not the sentiment of existence, with its severing of erotic fantasy and desire, but the sentiment of otherness, with its apparitions of the saving beloved. In Keats the desire for the "phantom of delight" does not give way before what Grossman calls the pressures and the "criteria of civility."

We may think of Keats's well-known tactile imagery as notations of achieved intimacy, of the return to the beloved which is simultaneously the arrival at a port beyond prosaic death: the taste, the kiss, the embrace, the offered hand. If "death is the great divorcer for ever," as he says passionately about his Italian separation from Fanny Brawne, then the poem can refer to the hope of the marriage, with its implications of communal ceremony and reassurance. This is the importance to Keats of the Psyche myth: the sensuality of the love of Eros and Psyche in darkness is necessary for desire but insufficient in the oblivion it predicts. The "blushes" in Keats's poetry indicate embarrassment in order to reinforce the poet's consciousness of the social immediacy of desire. The deferrals or apparent failures of his gestures at sexual intimacy—

> Pale were the sweet lips I saw,
> Pale were the lips I kiss'd, and fair the form
> I floated with, about that melancholy storm
>
> Faded the voice, warmth, whiteness, paradise—
>
> Their arms embraced, and their pinions too;
> Their lips touch'd not, but had not bade adieu,
> As if disjoined by soft-handed slumber,
> And ready still past kisses to outnumber
> At tender eye-dawn of aurorean love . . .
>
> Bold Lover, never, never canst thou kiss,
> Though winning near the goal . . .

—mean that he refuses to let desire die by its own completion; its very achievement would signal its dissolution into ordinary experience. Its deferral makes it continue beyond darkness into hope, and by this extension desire becomes "heretical." [2]

Romantic poetry is filled with apparitions: Wordsworth's Lucy and cuckoo and solitary reaper, Coleridge's Geraldine and nightingale, Shelley's skylark, Keats's Psyche and nightingale. All refer, in their voice or aspect, to a subject for hope. (In Keats and Shelley, more doggedly than in Wordsworth, the passionate subjectivity of the poet converges—in the setting of intimacy—with the apparition.) All call up desire in the poet for the other who is, as Wordsworth says, "sweet" in its freedom. This is the implicitly feminist element in Romantic poetry. Thus the silencing of the feminine is incomplete and is partly a function of how wedded we are to the dominant traditions of reading Romantic poetry. An "apparition" of a woman may signify her permanent and desired insubstantiality or indicate that she contains, in hope and possibility, her own freedom; that the male fantasy may contain a similar hope.

Herein, moreover, lies the "heretical" definition of Beauty, which, says Walter Benjamin, is poetry's hermetic aspect. Beauty lights upon apparitions, veiled representations, to insure the existence and the possibility of a sweet otherness. No accident that Keats's favorite god is Hermes, who slips past borders of propriety and civility to offer the poet access to the apparition:

> So felt he, who first told, how Psyche went
> On the smooth wind to realms of wonderment;
> What Psyche felt, and Love, when their full lips
> First touch'd; . . .
>
> .   .   .   .   .   .
>
> So did he feel, who pull'd the boughs aside,
> That we might look into a forest wide,
> To catch a glimpse of Fauns, and Dryades
> Coming with softest rustle through the trees. . . .

Notes
Index

[Notes]

[1] *Romanticism, and Passion, and Beauty*

1. Walter Pater, "Wordsworth," *Appreciations* (London: Macmillan, 1889), 37–63.

2. George Edward Woodberry, "Wordsworth," *The Torch* (New York: McClure, Phillips, 1905), 167.

3. Jean-Jacques Rousseau, *Reveries of the Solitary Walker*, trans. Peter France (New York: Penguin Books, 1979), 116.

4. *The Poetry and Prose of William Blake*, ed. David V. Erdman and Harold Bloom (Garden City: Doubleday, 1970), 45.

5. Ibid., 461.

6. Leo Tolstoy, *What Is Art?* trans. Aylmer Maude (London: Walter Scott, 1900), 40.

7. *Philosophies of Art and Beauty*, ed. Albert Hofstadter and Richard Kuhns (New York: Random House, 1964), 62.

8. Octavio Paz, *The Bow and the Lyre*, trans. Ruth L. C. Simms (New York: McGraw-Hill, 1973), 15; *Children of the Mire*, trans. Rachel Phillips (Cambridge: Harvard UP, 1974), 110.

9. Herbert Marcuse, "The Affirmative Character of Culture," *Negations*, trans. Jeremy J. Shapiro (Boston: Beacon Press, 1968), 115.

10. Herbert Marcuse, *The Aesthetic Dimension*, trans. and rev. Herbert Marcuse and Erica Sherover (Boston: Beacon Press, 1978), 62–63.

11. Roland Barthes, "Diderot, Brecht, Eisenstein," *The Responsibility of Forms*, trans. Richard Howard (New York: Hill and Wang, 1985), 92–93.

12. Marcuse, *Aesthetic Dimension*, 64–65.

13. Bertolt Brecht, *Poems 1913–1956*, ed. John Willett and Ralph Manheim (New York: Methuen, 1976), 482–83.

14. Allen Grossman, "Hart Crane and Poetry: A Consideration of Crane's Intense Poetics with Reference to 'The Return,'" *ELH*, 48 (1981), 873.

15. Quoted in John Berger, *The Sense of Sight* (New York: Pantheon Books, 1985), 272.

16. Friedrich Schiller, *On the Aesthetic Education of Man*, trans. Reginald Snell (New York: Frederick Ungar, 1954), 51–52.

17. Theodor W. Adorno, "Cultural Criticism and Society," *Prisms*, trans. Samuel Weber and Shierry Weber (Cambridge: MIT Press, 1981), 29.

[2] *The Sentiment of Existence—I*

1. Rousseau, *Solitary Walker*, 89. The idea and the phrase in a slightly different form also appear in Rousseau's *The Confessions*, trans. J. M. Cohen (New York: Penguin Books, 1954), 19 and 63. In addition, William Wordsworth touches on this idea in book II of *The Prelude*: "I have endeavoured to display the means / Whereby the infant sensibility, / Great birthright of our being, was in me / Augmented and sustained." *The Prelude 1799, 1805, 1850*, ed. Jonathan Wordsworth, M. H. Abrams, and Stephen Gill (New York: W. W. Norton, 1979), I, 265–68.

[3] *The Sentiment of Existence—II*

1. Rousseau, *Confessions*, Book 12, 594; *Solitary Walker*, 88–89.
2. William Wordsworth, "Preface to the Lyrical Ballads, with Pastoral and Other Poems (1802)," *William Wordsworth: The Poems*, Vol. 1, ed. John O. Hayden (New Haven: Yale UP, 1977), 880.

[4] *The Sentiment of Existence and the Shock from Nature*

1. Schiller, "Twenty-first Letter," *Aesthetic Education*, 100–101. Schiller, in a discussion of the "determinability" of the human mind in its aesthetic and moral capabilities, here distinguishes essentially negative or "deficient" determinability ("empty infinity") from what he considers to be its proper counterpart—aesthetic freedom of determination, or "filled infinity."
2. Benjamin, "Some Motifs in Baudelaire," *Illuminations*, 162–67, passim; Charles Baudelaire, "A une passante," *The Flowers of Evil*, ed. Marthiel Mathews and Jackson Mathews, rev. ed. (New York: New Directions, 1955), 237:

> La rue assourdissante autour de moi hurlait.
> Longue, mince, en grand deuil, douleur majestueuse,
> Une femme passa. . . .
>
> . . . .
>
> Moi, je buvais, crispé comme un extravagant,
> Dans son oeil, ciel livide où germe l'ouragan,
> La douceur qui fascine et le plaisir qui tue.

(Amid the deafening traffic of the town,
Tall, slender, in deep mourning, with majesty,
A woman passed. . . .

.   .   .   .

And I drank, trembling as a madman thrills,
From her eyes, ashen sky where brooded storm,
The softness that fascinates, the pleasure that kills.)

3. Rousseau, *Solitary Walker*, 39.
4. "The Fight," *The Complete Works of William Hazlitt*, ed. P. P. Howe (London: J. M. Dent and Sons, 1930–34), Vol. 17, 82–83.

[5] *The Romantic Poet as Orestes*

1. Schiller, "Ninth Letter," *Aesthetic Education*, 51–52.

[6] *Schiller: Beauty and Desire*

1. Friedrich Schiller, *Sämtliche Werke*, Vol. 5 (Munich: Carl Hanser Verlag, 1967), 573.
2. Schiller, *Aesthetic Education*, 128–29.

[7] *Rousseau's Ambivalence about Passion*

1. Jean-Jacques Rousseau, *Emile*, trans. Barbara Foxley (London: J. M. Dent; New York: Dutton, 1974), 173.
2. Ibid., 172.

[8] *The Lively Pleasure*

1. Rousseau, *Confessions*, Book 6, 240–41.

[9] *"The Grand Elementary Principle of Pleasure"*

1. Lionel Trilling, "The Fate of Pleasure," *Beyond Culture: Essays on Literature and Learning* (New York: Viking Press, 1968), 57–87, passim.

[10] *Blake's Joseph and Mary*

1. William Blake, "Jerusalem, the Emanation of the Giant Albion," *The Poems of William Blake* (complete), ed. W. H. Stevenson, text David V. Erdman (London: Longman, 1971), plate 61, 753–54.

[11] *Two Passages from Joubert*

1. Joseph Joubert, *The Notebooks of Joseph Joubert: A Selection*, ed. and trans. Paul Auster (San Francisco: North Point Press, 1983), 51.
2. Dorothy Wordsworth, *Recollections of a Tour Made in Scotland (1803)*, *Journals of Dorothy Wordsworth*, Vol. 1, ed. E. de Selincourt (London: Macmillan, 1941), 320.

[12] *"Bright Star" on the Lawn*

1. John Keats, "Bright Star! Would I were steadfast as thou art," *The Poems of John Keats* (complete), ed. Miriam Allott (New York: Longman, 1970), 736–39.

[13] *Beauty and Anxiety*

1. Rainer Maria Rilke, *Letters on Cézanne*, ed. Clara Rilke, trans. Joel Agee (New York: Fromm International, 1985), 10.

[15] *Rousseau: Calm, Solitude, and Power*

1. Rousseau, Solitary Walker, 134.

[16] *"Emmeline" and Resistance in Wordsworth's Lyrics*

1. Matthew Arnold, ed., *Poems of Wordsworth* (London, 1879), xxii.

[17] *The Scene—I*

1. Rousseau, *Confessions*, Part II. This observation reflects the period in Rousseau's life when he feels as if the larger social world is entangling and suffocating him.

2. Johann Wolfgang von Goethe, "The Sorrows of Young Werther," *The Sorrows of Young Werther and Selected Writings*, ed. Hermann J. Weigand, trans. Catherine Hutter (New York: New American Library, 1962), 127.

[18] *The Scene—II*

1. Ann Radcliffe, *The Italian or The Confessional of the Black Penitents: A Romance*, ed. Frederick Garber (London: Oxford UP, 1968), 412–15, passim. The last chapter (chapter 12) of Radcliffe's romance is set at a villa near Naples. The author describes the idyllic landscape at length and in extravagant terms: the land is Italy, but the style of the gardens, lawns, groves, etc., is described as "of England and of the present day." In this Edenic setting the principals of the adventure—Vivaldi, Paulo, and Ellena—"rejoice" in their present and future happiness ("who would have thought we should ever be let loose again . . . [that] we should ever know what it is to be happy!"). The novel ends in a chorus of voices shouting, "O Giorno Felice!"

2. See Max Horkheimer and Theodor W. Adorno, *The Dialectic of Enlightenment*, trans. John Cumming (New York: Continuum, 1972), 30: "[In enlightened thought] the transcendental subject of cognition is apparently abandoned as the last reminiscence of subjectivity and is replaced by the much smoother work of automatic control mechanisms . . . self preservation repeatedly culminates in the choice between survival and destruction. . . . The formalism of this principle and of the entire logic in which form it is established derives from the opacity and complexity of interests in a society in which the maintenance of forms and the preservation of individuals coincide only by chance."

3. Mary Wollstonecraft, *Maria; Or the Wrongs of Woman* (New York: W. W. Norton, 1975), 23.

4. See Stendhal's comment that beauty is "une promesse de bonheur," quoted by Herbert Marcuse in *Negations*, 115.

[20] *An Idyll of Liberty*

1. *Coleridge; The Critical Heritage* (London: Routledge and Kegan Paul, 1970), 50.

[21] *"Colouring of Imagination"*

1. Edmund Burke, *Reflections on the Revolution in France* (New York: Penguin Books, 1979), 171.

2. Marilyn Butler, ed., *Burke, Paine, Godwin and the Revolution Controversy* (Cambridge: Cambridge UP, 1984), 74.

[22] *Thelwall, Coleridge, and Domestic Poetry*

1. John Thelwall (1764–1834), "Poems Chiefly written in Retirement," included in a volume entitled *John Thelwall: Ode to Science, John Gilpin's Ghost, Poems, The Trident of Albion*, ed. Donald H. Reiman (New York: Garland, 1978), 136–39.
2. Ibid., 138.
3. "To the Infant Hampden—Written during a sleepless night. Derby, October 1797," *John Thelwall*, 141. See also Coleridge, "Frost at Midnight," lines 4–7: "The inmates of my cottage, all at rest, / Have left me to that solitude, which suits / Abstruser musings: Save that at my side / My cradled infant slumbers peacefully . . ." and lines 48–51: "My babe so beautiful! it thrills my heart / With tender gladness, thus to look at thee, / And think that thou shalt learn far other lore, / And in far other scenes!" See also Coleridge, "The Nightingale," lines 106–10: "It is a father's tale: But if that Heaven / Should give me life, his childhood shall grow up / familiar with these songs that with the night / He may associate Joy—Once more, farewell, / Sweet Nightingale! once more, my friends! farewell."
4. "Maria: A Fragment," *John Thelwall*, 138.
5. "Gloucestershire," *John Thelwall*, 138.
6. "Hampden," *John Thelwall*, 141.

[23] *Thelwall, Coleridge, and Nature's Rescue*

1. S. T. Coleridge cited by Donald Reiman in *John Thelwall*, Introduction, iv.
2. William Hazlitt cited by Donald Reiman in Introduction, *John Thelwall*, ix.

[24] *Thelwall: Denying Politics, Creating the Romantic Self*

1. "July 27, 1830," *Specimens of the Table Talk of the Late Samuel Taylor Coleridge*, Vol. 1 (New York: Harper and Brothers, 1835), 129.
2. "Lines Written at Bridgewater, in Somersetshire, on the 27th of July, 1797, during a long excursion, in quest of a peacefull retreat," *John Thelwall*, 132.
3. "Prefatory Memoir," *John Thelwall*, i–ii.
4. "The Reply," *John Thelwall*, 135.

[26] *Judgment and Disinterestedness—II: The Walker*

1. Franz Kafka, "Passers-by," *The Complete Stories*, ed. Nahum N. Glatzer (New York: Schocken Books, 1983), 388.
2. Robert Jay Lifton, *Boundaries: Psychological Man in Revolution* (New York: Random House, 1967), 31–33. See also William Wordsworth, *1805 Prelude*, ix, 935–36, in which Vaudracour is described thus: "in those solitary shades / His days he wasted, an imbecile mind."

[28] *Lucy and TV*

1. William S. Burroughs, "Creative Reading," *The Adding Machine: Selected Essays* (London: Seaver Books, 1985, 1986), 44–45.

[32] *A Moment of Recalcitrance in* The Prelude

1. Karen Horney, M.D., "The Problem of the Monogomous Ideal," in *Feminine Psychology*, ed. Harold Kelman, M.D. (New York: W. W. Norton, 1967), 85–86.
2. "Lesbia," in "The Poems of Gaius" Valerius Catullus," *Catullus, Tibullus and Pervigilium Veneris*, trans. F. W. Cornish (Cambridge: Loeb Classical Library; Harvard UP, 1962), 5, lines 7–13, 6–9.

> da mi basia mille, deinde centum,
> dein mille altera, dein secunda centum,
> deinde usque altera mille, deinde centum
> dein, cum milia multa fecerimus,
> conturbabimus illa, ne sciamus,
> aut nequis malus invidere possit
> cum tantum sciat esse basiorum.
>
> (Give me a thousand kisses, then a hundred then
> another thousand, then a second hundred, then yet
> another thousand, then a hundred. Then, when we
> have made up many thousands, we will confuse our
> counting, that we may not know the reckoning, nor
> any malicious person blight them with evil eye, when
> he knows that our kisses are so many.)

[33] *A Question about the Form of This Essay*

1. Paul de Man, *The Rhetoric of Romanticism* (New York: Columbia UP, 1984), viii.

[35] *"Klopstock"*

1. Goethe, *The Sorrows of Young Werther*, 41.
2. Letter 62, August 6, 1800, *The Complete Works and Letters of Charles Lamb* (New York: Modern Library, 1935), 660.

[36] *"Either . . . Or"*

1. Goethe, *The Sorrows of Young Werther*, 55.
2. Ibid.
3. Marilyn Butler, *Romantics, Rebels and Reactionaries: English Literature and Its Background, 1760–1830* (New York: Oxford UP, 1981). See especially "Conclusion: The Question of Romanticism in England," 178–87, passim.
4. Geoffrey H. Hartman, *Wordsworth's Poetry, 1787–1814* (New Haven: Yale UP, 1964), 11.

[37] *Conversion*

1. Rousseau, *Solitary Walker*, 117.

[38] *The Isolate Feminine Voice*

1. Mary Wollstonecraft, *Maria*, 153.

[40] *Wollstonecraft's Animadversion on Rousseau's Sensibility*

1. Wollstonecraft, *A Critical Edition of Mary Wollstonecraft's "A Vindication of the Rights of Women: With Strictures on Political and Moral Subjects,"* ed. Ulrich H. Hardt (Troy: Whitson, 1928), 198–99.
2. See *The Poems of Gray, Collins, and Goldsmith*, ed. Roger Lonsdale (London: Longmans, 1969), 462 for Cooper's remarks.

3. From the Notebook, c. 1791–92: LI "Several Questions Answered," lines 11–14, *Poems of William Blake*, 167.

4. Wollstonecraft, *Vindication*, 199.

5. Ibid.

6. Ibid., 200.

[41] *Charles Lamb's* Rosamund Gray

1. The editions referred to and upon which the following discussion is based are as follows: Charles Lamb, *A Tale of Rosamund Gray and Old Blind Margaret*, introd. R. Brimely Johnson (London: Golden Cokerel Press, 1928). This edition, on page ix, announces that it was printed from: "*A Tale of Rosamund Gray and Old Blind Margaret*. Charles Lamb. London, printed for Lee and Hurst, No. 32, Paternoster Row. 1798, 12 months., 134 pp." Bernardin Saint Pierre, *Paul and Virginia*, trans. Helen Maria Williams (London: John Sharpe, 1829). As the preface to this volume indicates, the translation by Helen Maria Williams was made "amidst the horrors of Robespierre's tyranny" and is dated "Paris, June, 1795."

2. Lamb, *Rosamund Gray*, 65.

3. Hazlitt, "My First Acquaintance with Poets," *Complete Works*, Vol. 17, 122.

[42] *Disappointment*

1. Quoted in James Chandler, *Wordsworth's Second Nature: A Study of Poetry and Politics* (Chicago: U of Chicago P, 1984), 19.

2. Ibid., 12–25, passim.

3. For both "My First Acquaintance with Poets" and "On Going a Journey," see *Complete Works*, Vol. 17, 106–22, and Vol. 8, 181–89.

4. "Acquaintance," *Complete Works*, Vol. 17, 110.

5. "The Spirit of the Age: Mr. Wordsworth," *Complete Works*, Vol. 11, 88.

6. Dante Alighieri, "Inferno," *The Divine Comedy*, trans. Carlyle-Wicksteed (New York: Modern Library, 1950), canto 1, 11–16, passim.

7. Hazlitt, "On Going a Journey," Vol. 8, 183.

8. Ibid., 187.

9. Ibid., 186–87.

[43] *Demystifying Romanticism: A Diary Entry*

1. Rilke, *Letters on Cézanne*, 50.

2. Lionel Trilling, "Why We Read Jane Austen," *The Last Decade: Essays and Reviews, 1965–75*, ed. Diana Trilling (New York: Harcourt, Brace, Jovanovich, 1979), 219.

3. Lionel Trilling, "Mansfield Park," *The Opposing Self: Nine Essays in Criticism* (New York: Harcourt, Brace, Jovanovich, 1978), 191.

[44] *Crystallization*

1. Stendhal, *Love*, trans. Gilbert Sale and Suzanne Sale (New York: Penguin Books, 1975), 208.

2. Ibid., 209.

3. Ibid.

4. Simone de Beauvoir, *The Second Sex*, trans. and ed. H. M. Parshley (New York: Bantam, 1952), 232.

5. Stendhal, *Love*, 45.

[45] *Adolphe: The Contingencies of Love*

1. Benjamin Constant, "Adolphe," *Adolphe and The Red Notebook* (New York: Signet, 1959), 73.

2. Ibid., 89.

3. Ibid., 68.

[50] *Dorothy Wordsworth's Scottish* Recollections

1. Wollstonecraft, *Maria*, 51.

2. Mary Wollstonecraft, *Letters Written during a Short Residence in Sweden, Norway, and Denmark*, ed. Carol H. Poston (Lincoln: U of Nebraska P, 1976). This work is a series of twenty-five letters written to Wollstonecraft's lover, Gilbert Imlay, from Scandinavia, where she had gone as his business envoy during the summer of 1795. Although intended initially as personal correspondence, the *Letters* are also the productions of an impassioned social critic and advocate of the rights of women who was in addition quite familiar with the genre of eighteenth-century travel literature. The letters contain the astute social and cultural observations of a skillful stylist as well as of a political radical. Wollstonecraft's chronicle of her journey through the Scandinavian countries was published in 1769 by Joseph Johnson under the present title.

3. Virginia Woolf, "Four Figures: IV Dorothy Wordsworth," *The Second Common Reader* (New York: Harcourt, Brace, and World, 1960), 155.

4. Dorothy Wordsworth, *Recollections*, 206.

5. Ibid., 219.

6. Ibid., 221.

7. For another reference to an "interstitial site," see Roland Barthes' "Kristeva's Semiotike," *The Rustle of Language*, trans. Richard Howard (New York: Hill and Wang, 1986), 171.

[51] *Childhood, or The Suppression of Adolescence*

1. Hazlitt, *Complete Works*, Vol. 4, 248–51.

[52] *Burke, De Quincey, Stendhal*

1. Thomas De Quincey, *Confessions of an English Opium Eater and Other Writings*, ed. Aileen Ward (New York: Carroll and Graf, 1985), 120.

[53] *The Romantic Essay: Cultural Criticism and the Romantic Ego*

1. Charles Lamb, "Blakesmoor in H . . . shire," *Complete Works*, 139.

2. Ibid.

3. Lamb, "A Dissertation upon Roast Pig," *Complete Works*, 110.

4. Goethe, *Goethe on Art*, trans. and ed. John Gage (Berkeley: U of California P, 1980), 108. In the passage in which this statement appears, Goethe relates how he had visited the Strasbourg Minster "full of common notions of good taste" and was prepared heartily to disapprove of that Gothic building "smothered with ornament." Instead, he found that the structure was "composed of a thousand harmonizing details" which reminded him of the "eternal works" of nature "perfectly formed down to the meanest thread" (106–8).

5. Lamb, "The Convalescent," *Complete Works*, 164–67, passim.

[54] *Hazlitt's "The Fight"*

1. Herschel M. Sikes, ed., *The Hazlitt Sampler* (Gloucester: Peter Smith, 1969), 231.

2. Hazlitt, *Complete Works*, Vol. 11, 95.

3. Ibid., Vol. 17, 82–83.

4. David Bromwich, *Hazlitt: The Mind of a Critic* (New York: Oxford UP, 1983), 113.

5. Hazlitt, *Complete Works*, Vol. 17, 73.

6. Bromwich, *Hazlitt*, 436–37.

{55} *Haidee's Father*

1. Robert Gittings, ed., *Letters of John Keats* (New York: Oxford UP, 1970), 118.

{57} *Return: The Sentiment of Otherness*

1. Dorothy Van Ghent, *Keats: The Myth of the Hero*, ed. Jeffrey Cane Robinson (Princeton: Princeton UP, 1983), 142.

2. Giles Gunn, *The Culture of Criticism and the Criticism of Culture* (New York: Oxford UP, 1987), 179.

[*Index*]